National Gallery of Art

WASHINGTON

International Standard Book Number: 0-8109-1364-X (H.C.)/0-8109-2185-5 (pb.)
Library of Congress Catalogue Card Number: 78-23284
Concise Edition 1979

The lines quoted on page 158 are reprinted from *Duino Elegies*, by Rainer Maria Rilke, translated
by J.B. Leishman and Stephen Spender, with permission of W.W. Norton & Co., Inc., copyright 1939
by W.W. Norton & Co., Inc. Copyright renewed 1967 by Stephen Spender and J.B. Leishman.

Printed and bound in Japan

JOHN WALKER DIRECTOR EMERITUS

National G

West Building, exterior view

Introduction by John Walker, *Director Emeritus*, and J. Carter Brown, *Director*

allery of Art
WASHINGTON

East Building, exterior view

HARRY N. ABRAMS, INC., PUBLISHERS, NEW YORK

The West Building

by John Walker, *Director Emeritus*

The National Gallery of Art comprises two buildings, both in the shadow of the Capitol, one which opened in 1941 and the other in 1978. Although the addition of 1978, known as the East Building, is smaller in its outside dimensions, it contains four exhibition levels rather than two, as well as eight floors for the library and the office area; consequently the usable space in both is roughly equal. Their architectural idioms, however, are quite different, reflecting the differences in taste of Andrew Mellon and his son, Paul. The earlier West Building was designed by the last outstanding master of Neo-Classicism, John Russell Pope. The new addition, a consummate example of contemporary style, is the work of I.M. Pei. The change in taste between the thirties and the seventies, as seen in these two edifices, is a striking illustration of the mutations of fashion. Yet the two buildings are remarkably harmonious. They have been related by the use of the same material, a rose Tennessee marble, by their axial placement, and by the maintenance of a uniform height for various components. Each is, in a way, expressive of its contents: the Neo-Classical building, of paintings from Duccio to Cézanne and sculpture from Nino Pisano to Maillol; the modern addition, of the work of subsequent artists.

John Russell Pope created the noblest tribute of the twentieth century to Classicism. He was a martyr to his desire to erect one last monument to that great artistic tradition, which began with the Greeks and Romans and continued through the Renaissance until its final extinction in our own time. Knowing himself desperately ill, Pope worked feverishly at his designs. His doctor told him in the spring of 1937 that he had cancer and that an immediate operation offered a good chance of survival; otherwise the disease would be terminal in six months. In order to continue working on the drawings for the Gallery, Pope refused the operation. Within six months he was dead. Just twenty-four hours earlier, Andrew Mellon had died. But the plans for the Gallery were completed organizationally and architecturally.

The exterior was influenced by George Hadfield's Old District Court House erected in 1820. On the east and west ends are lofty portals and on the north and south monumental Ionic porticoes. Otherwise the exterior is adorned only with niches and pilasters, and the beauty of the building lies in its marble masonry, delicately rose in color, and in its harmony of proportion.

Pope was an architect preeminent in his ability to handle classical forms dramatically. As the main feature of the Gallery he designed a rotunda with a great coffered dome upheld by towering columns of green-black marble. This central area, in its proportions, its concept of space, its classical orders, is a free adaptation of the interior of the Pantheon in Rome. Joined to the rotunda by halls for monumental sculpture are two garden courts where changing exhibitions of flowers, grown in the Gallery's greenhouses, are always displayed. Around these architectural features are grouped the rooms for paintings and smaller sculpture.

The building was intended to satisfy an often unrecognized desire on the part of the public. In this country there is a lack of the magnificent churches, public buildings, and palaces of Europe; Americans living for the most part in apartments and small houses feel the need for buildings more sumptuous, more spacious, and less utilitarian than their everyday surroundings. The satisfaction of this desire has a psychological value as definite as it is difficult to analyze. From architecture that has dignity, splendor, permanence, people seem to gain an enhancement of their own personalities. There can be no doubt that, disregarding the collections, visitors receive great pleasure from the National Gallery simply as architecture.

But there is always a danger that the museum building will dominate its contents. This, I believe, the National Gallery of Art has avoided. Rather than clutter up the painting and sculpture galleries with antique furniture, statuary, tapestries, and other decorative arts, as is the practice in some museums, in the National Gallery the picture galleries are galleries of pictures; the sculpture galleries, galleries of sculpture. Commodious sofas there are; but these are to rest the weary, not to indicate the type of settle used by Lorenzo the Magnificent.

To avoid monotony and to harmonize with the styles of painting, different backgrounds are used for the different rooms: plaster for the early Italian, Flemish, and German pictures; damask for later Italian paintings; oak paneling for Rubens, van Dyck, Rembrandt, and the other Dutch; and painted paneling for the French, English, and American canvases. A suggestion of the architectural styles prevalent when these schools flourished is indicated in wainscoting, moldings, and overdoors.

But the basic goal has always been to permit the visitor a concentrated and undistracted scrutiny of each work of art. Therefore, the pictures are hung twice as far apart as one usually sees them in other galleries—a method of installation which has been generally commended though very little imitated. In many rooms paneling is used to achieve greater isolation for each painting. The separation thus affords a second frame, so to speak, which more than compensates for any loss of flexibility.

Thus the whole installation of the Gallery has been determined by a basic assumption: that the work of art is not a specimen, not primarily a historical document, but a source of pleasure. An art gallery and a concert hall have much in common: one affords delight to the eye, the other to the ears.

The museum director and the conductor of an orchestra are also comparable: both present as satisfactorily as possible the works of others, both have an interpretative function to perform, much greater, of course, in the case of the conductor. But the museum director has a further responsibility which the conductor is spared. He must preserve what he presents. In recent years this task of preservation has been immeasurably aided by air conditioning. The National Gallery is the largest completely air-conditioned art museum in the world; and the system works so well that atmospheric variations can be controlled to within five degrees of relative humidity. This stability has proved a vital factor in increasing the longevity of paintings, especially those executed on wood. For all pictures are vulnerable to fluctuations of humidity. These changes cause the support—the substance on which the picture is painted—to expand and contract at a rate different from the expansion and contraction of the surface of the picture. Consequently, blisters and cracks occur, which in turn cause the pigment to flake and chip away. The National Gallery of Art has one of the largest collections in the world of early Italian paintings, which are especially fragile. Yet, because of the stability of the atmosphere, almost no restoration has been required once these pictures have grown accustomed to their environment.

Before I retired in 1969, it became apparent that space in the original building had been used up. We could not show all the works of art we had been given, the library could not expand, the staff was cramped. Since neither we nor the architect we chose wanted to deface the symmetry of the existing building by tacking on an appendage, a second, separate building was essential. That it could be erected was owing to the foresight of Andrew Mellon, who stipulated at the time of his original gift of the building and his own great collection that an additional area on the Mall be reserved by Congress for the Gallery's future expansion. This plot, the most prominent unused site left in Washington, lay between the original building and the Capitol. Thirty years passed, and it remained unoccupied. Meanwhile the Gallery's claim to an invaluable piece of real estate had become so tenuous that there was doubt in 1967 as to whether Congress would enact the necessary legislation to permit its use. Fortunately, however, I was able to tell the Committee on Public Buildings, much to their astonishment, that the money to erect the new building would be provided privately. Their relief on hearing this assured their concurrence, and with the support of President Johnson a bill authorizing the National Gallery's expansion was passed unanimously.

I retired from the Gallery shortly thereafter and my successor, J. Carter Brown, has been entirely responsible for the East Building.

West Building, interior view

The East Building

by J. Carter Brown, *Director*

After an analysis of the site and its potentials by Pietro Belluschi, himself not a candidate for the commission, the architect I.M. Pei was selected. The Trustees asked for a solution that would take maximum advantage of the site, as this represented the last opportunity the Gallery would ever have to expand into contiguous space.

Pei utilized the site fully by fitting a trapezoidal plan on the trapezoidal plot; this he divided diagonally into two complementary triangles, one devoted to exhibition space and the other to the Center for Advanced Study in the Visual Arts. Thus, from the beginning, two sets of functions were envisaged for the East Building. The exhibition area is designed to accommodate changing exhibitions and provide for the growth of the permanent collections. This is particularly necessary, as the survey of Western painting and sculpture that the National Gallery offers will continue to grow into the twentieth century and beyond. The Study Center provides offices for scholars, major library and photographic archives, and office space for Gallery administration.

Mr. Pei and his associates started with an analysis of the Gallery's needs, of which one of the most important was the maintenance of a homogenous environment for delicate works of art when they had to be transported to any point in the new complex. It is an interesting commentary on the modern assumption of progress that when the mechanical engineers were given the specifications that the new air-conditioning system would have to meet to match the old, they found that the best system yet devised was essentially the same as the original one, itself one of the earliest installations of its scale ever to be made. In fact, valuable space in the new construction was saved by simply adding compressors in the basement of the earlier building, so that the entire new complex is serviced from one central point.

The architect gave early consideration to the problem of the new building's responsibility to its urban site. The building is at the juncture of Pennsylvania Avenue and the Mall, the two major axes designed by Pierre L'Enfant in the eighteenth century. Its exterior had to relate to Pennsylvania Avenue, with its Federal Triangle cornice line, the highest in the city, and in scale it had to be commensurate with the neighboring museums of History and Technology and Natural History, the earlier National Gallery building, and the Capitol itself. The intersection of Pennsylvania and Constitution avenues had previously been spatially undefined, but now in accordance with Pei's vision the East Building of the Gallery heads the parade of monumental federal structures leading from the Capitol to the White House and the Washington Monument.

Another challenge facing the architect was that of relating the new building to the older one across Fourth Street. An early decision was made to construct it of exactly the same rose-colored Tennessee marble. To make it still more evident that the old and new structures form one complex, Pei projected the axis of the Pope building through the new galleries, and astride this axis, connecting the buildings, he designed a plaza which links the facades firmly together, overcoming the intrusion of Fourth Street. In many ways this was a virtuoso solution, in that the center of the new site is considerably south of that axis, and most of the area covered by the new building is asymmetrical in relation to the old.

The outdoor plaza is paved in the European manner with concentric fans of Belgian block granite. In the center, as a visual focus, is a cluster of great glass tetrahedrons, flanked to the north by a line of fountain jets from which water rushes down an open slide to form a waterfall in the underground concourse below. The tetrahedrons provide daylight to this below-grade section of the connecting link.

The visitor coming through the underground concourse from the original building will find a lively area equipped with a "sidewalk" café, a large self-service facility, including a snack bar, a museum shop, and, at the end, a moving walkway angled upward, leading directly into a lower lobby of the East Building. On that level there is access to a large and a small auditorium and a large, flexible space for temporary exhibitions.

Visitors entering the East Building from the out-

East Building, interior view

door plaza pass through a broad, low-ceilinged reception area into a great glass-roofed courtyard, opening to four levels of courts or balconies. Besides providing a spacious setting for sculpture, the space, with its greenery and sense of openness to the sky, creates a transition from the plaza and the Mall park, and acts as a natural orientation space. Open stairs and escalators lead to the various exhibition levels, housed in three gallery towers connected by bridge galleries and access bridges. A terrace café on the fourth floor provides visitors with a convenient place to rest.

The Gallery spaces offer a great variety of environments for changing exhibitions of art of all periods, and for future additions to the permanent collection. Some of these are extremely intimate, recalling the scale of a domestic residence. Others have daylight ceilings capable of adjustment up to 35 feet high. Thus the walls, and in many cases the ceilings of the spaces in which the works of art are exhibited, can be manipulated by the Gallery staff to tune them to specific works of art to be presented.

The second triangle of the East Building, housing the Center for Advanced Study with its library and offices, has its own entrance off the plaza. At the heart of this building is a lofty reading room with adjoining book stacks. There are large areas above and below ground for a photographic archive, reference works, and storage. Space has been provided for three hundred thousand volumes, with room for further expansion.

Duccio di Buoninsegna

(SIENESE, ACTIVE 1278–1318/19)

1   THE CALLING OF THE APOSTLES PETER AND ANDREW

The greatest single creation of the Byzantine School was painted not in Byzantium but in Siena. The Byzantine tradition culminated in the *Maestà—The Virgin in Majesty*—painted for the Cathedral of Siena between 1308 and 1311 by Duccio di Buoninsegna. This altarpiece is a compendium of all that men had learned during a thousand years about the craft of painting. Within the Byzantine style there is no more skillful use of line, pattern, and composition, no finer example of dramatic power and significant characterization.

Duccio's altarpiece was not only the most perfect expression of medieval painting, it also contained the seeds of future development. In *The Calling of the Apostles Peter and Andrew*, a panel which once formed part of the predella of the *Maestà*, there is evidence that the hieratic rigidity of the Byzantine style has changed. There is a tender awareness of human life, of its daily activity. The apostles busily netting their fish, and the aquatic life itself, open new vistas in art. This rudimentary naturalism was stimulated by the growing popularity of the Franciscan interest in nature. But the figure of Christ has still the austerity of Byzantine art. The edge of His robe is still touched with gold, which, like a flash of lightning, sets Him apart from common humanity. When the *Maestà* was completed, the Sienese realized that their altarpiece was, of its type, the supreme masterpiece of the age. A great procession was formed to carry it in triumph to the high altar of the Cathedral, and a whole day was devoted to prayers and hymns to the Virgin.

Duccio's masterwork was dismembered in 1771 and again in 1878, but most of it may still be seen in the Museo dell'Opera del Duomo in Siena, where it remains one of the principal treasures of the city. Ten sections of the predella were dispersed to England and the United States, and two of these, the one reproduced here and the *Nativity with the Prophets Isaiah and Ezekiel*, are now in the National Gallery of Art.

Collections: Cathedral of Siena; Robert H. and Evelyn Benson, London; Clarence H. Mackay, Roslyn, New York. *Samuel H. Kress Collection*, 1939. Painted between 1308 and 1311. Wood, 17⅛ x 18⅛" (43.5 x 46 cm.).

Giotto

(FLORENTINE, 1266?–1337)

2 MADONNA AND CHILD

Duccio sums up the past; Giotto foretells the future. Both artists typify the spirit of the cities in which they lived. Siena was conservative, sophisticated, overrefined; Florence was experimental, vigorous, dynamic. Duccio's style was the flowering of an ancient tradition, but Giotto's paintings, based on study of the human form and stimulated by intellectual curiosity, tore apart the formulas of the immediate past. Duccio developed the Eastern elements of Byzantine art—line, pattern, and composition on a flat plane. Giotto emphasized instead form, mass, and volume—the almost forgotten tradition of classical painting.

To appreciate the difference between these two approaches to painting, compare the figures in *The Calling of the Apostles Peter and Andrew* by Duccio, on the preceding page, and the figures of the *Madonna and Child* by Giotto. One feels intuitively something like a difference in specific gravity, as though Duccio's figures were made of aluminum and Giotto's of lead. It was Giotto's passion for solidity that determined the appearance of his figures, that caused him to depict large-boned, massive models. He willingly sacrificed superficial physical beauty to convey more intensely physical existence. This *Madonna and Child*, which may once have formed part of a celebrated altarpiece painted by Giotto for the Church of Santa Croce in Florence, is typical. It seems carved from a monolith as solid as a piece of granite. Every device is used to enhance the feeling of substance. Look, for instance, at the powerful rendering of the hands, the thickness and roundness of the fingers, the sense of existence conveyed by the manner in which the Christ Child grasps His Mother's forefinger.

Here Giotto has given us the essential quality of significant Florentine painting. Two hundred years later, Leonardo da Vinci was to define this quality in the following words: "The first object of the painter is to make a flat plane appear as a body in relief and projecting from that plane." In Giotto's work this suggestion of relief is rendered with a power that has never been surpassed.

Collections: Edouard-Alexandre Max, Paris; Henry Goldman, New York. *Samuel H. Kress Collection*, 1939. Painted probably between 1320 and 1330. Wood, 33⅝ x 24⅜" (85.5 x 62 cm.).

Fra Angelico and Fra Filippo Lippi

(FLORENTINE, ACTIVE 1417–1455; PROBABLY c.1406–1469)

3 THE ADORATION OF THE MAGI

This tondo ranks among the greatest Florentine paintings in the world. It is a climax of beauty, a summary in itself of the whole evolution of the Italian schools of painting in the first half of the fifteenth century, for it stands at a crossroads of art. The old style, the gay, colorful, fairy-tale painting of the Middle Ages, is ending in an outburst of splendor; and the new style, scientific in observation, studious in anatomy and perspective, realistic in its portrayal of life, is beginning its long development. Two harbingers of the future are the row of naked youths who watch the procession—an early indication of that preoccupation with human anatomy which was to obsess Italian artists until it reached its climax in Michelangelo and the Sistine Chapel—and the scene in the stable, which foretells the flowering of genre painting at a still later date. It is interesting to note the degree to which Florentine style for the next fifty years fell under the spell of the two monks who collaborated on this *Adoration of the Magi*. It is almost as though the Kress Collection tondo seeded a whole garden of art.

Berenson was the first to indicate the probable collaboration of two artists on this panel, concluding that it was probably left unfinished when Fra Angelico departed for Rome in 1445. Though he subsequently came to agree with most critics that the painting was largely by Fra Filippo Lippi, the influence of Fra Angelico is everywhere apparent, and in some cases his touch can be discerned. The tondo has been connected with an entry in the Medici inventory of 1492 made after the death of Lorenzo the Magnificent, which reads: "A tondo with its golden frame representing the Madonna and Our Lord and the Magi offering gifts, from the hand of Fra Giovanni [Fra Angelico] worth 100 florins." This was the highest price for a painting in the inventory.

Collections: Possibly Medici family; Guicciardini Palace, Florence; probably M. Dubois, Florence; William Coningham, London; Alexander Barker, London; Cook, Doughty House, Richmond, Surrey. *Samuel H. Kress Collection*, 1952. Painted c. 1445. Wood, diameter 54" (137.2 cm.).

Andrea del Castagno

(FLORENTINE, c. 1417/19–1457)

4 THE YOUTHFUL DAVID

One of the most vivid tales in Vasari's *Lives of the Painters* is the description of the brutal murder of Domenico Veneziano by his pupil Andrea del Castagno. We now know that Vasari's account is fictitious, for Domenico outlived his supposed murderer, but if a man's personality is reflected in his creations, then Vasari's characterization of Castagno is true. Truculence, bravado, a brutal power, these are the qualities that emanate from his work.

In his interpretation of the triumphant David, he is less aggressive, less savage than one would expect, but he displays, nevertheless, his power to overwhelm us with the sheer impact of emotion. The intense vitality of this heroic youth, vibrant with energy, anticipates the Romanticism of Géricault and Delacroix.

David is a symbolic figure, the ideal warrior, hard, resolute, conscious of his power, but conscious at the same time of its tragic implications. The head of the slain Goliath already lies at his feet. To the modern spectator this may seem an inconsistency in the sequence of events, but it did not disturb Castagno's contemporaries, for the picture is symbolic. It is not the representation of a historic occurrence. Consequently the act and the result of the act are shown simultaneously. For the meaning of the scene, the triumph of freedom over tyranny, could best be expressed this way.

The painting is on a leather shield and was probably carried in the processions which preceded the jousts, or tournaments, popular in the fifteenth century. Other ornamental shields exist, though they are rare, but this example is the only one by a great master that has survived.

Collections: Drury-Lowe, Locko Park, England. *Widener Collection*, 1942. Painted c. 1450. Leather, 45½ x 30¼" (115.5 x 77 cm.).

Botticelli

(FLORENTINE, 1444/45-1510)

5   THE ADORATION OF THE MAGI

With this *Adoration of the Magi* we reach the last quarter of the fifteenth century and the reign of Lorenzo de' Medici. Florence had become a center of Greek studies, Neoplatonism almost a religion. Refinement, a fastidious sensibility, a mood of poetic reverie had come into fashion. It was a time when pageants and ceremonials were popular and families took pride in having themselves portrayed as the principal actors in the dramas of Christianity. In the present painting, which Botticelli probably executed during his sojourn in Rome while he was working in the Sistine Chapel, the portraits have never been identified in spite of their incisive characterizations.

But the wonder of this *Adoration* does not consist so much in these portrait studies as in the subtle disposition of the figures, their vibrant movement, and their poetic setting. Amid the ruins of the classical world, symbolized by fragments of ancient architecture, the new order of Christianity is born. From the calmness of the central group, from the mystical yet human serenity of the Madonna and Child, movement radiates in waves of increasing activity through the gestures of awe and of prayer of the onlookers, and reaches a climax in the youthful grooms on the far right.

Beyond this human activity stretches a landscape suggestive of the serene spaces of the Campagna. It is impossible to let the eye travel into the tranquil beauty of this countryside without some relief of the spirit, some sense of refreshment and calm. The breadth, serenity, and restraint which are so conspicuous in this *Adoration* disappeared shortly thereafter from Botticelli's work. With the exile of the Medici he came under the spell of Savonarola, and his last years were overclouded by the feverish visions of the Dominican reformer.

Collections: Purchased in Rome by the engraver Peralli, it was acquired in 1808 for the Hermitage Gallery, Leningrad, by Czar Alexander I. *Andrew W. Mellon Collection*, 1937. Painted early 1480s. Wood, 27⅝ x 41" (71 x 103.5 cm.).

Leonardo da Vinci

(FLORENTINE, 1452–1519)

6 GINEVRA DE' BENCI

6a Leonardo da Vinci (Florentine, 1452–1519): Reverse of *Ginevra de' Benci*

On the reverse of the portrait of Ginevra de' Benci is the only painted still life by Leonardo da Vinci, if so heraldic a design can be thus designated.

The cost per square inch of paint of the portrait of Ginevra de' Benci is the greatest in the history of collecting. Why is the likeness of a young, seemingly disgruntled Florentine heiress so precious? Paintings by Leonardo da Vinci are indeed rare, but rarity in itself is only a cipher, dependent on the numbers that precede it. Furthermore, how can one be sure the picture is by that most extraordinary genius? True, all recent critics have agreed to this attribution, but on what is their judgment based? First, there is external evidence. We know from contemporary sources that Leonardo painted someone called Ginevra de' Benci. The juniper bush, so prominent in the portrait and repeated symbolically on the back, is considered to identify the sitter as that lady, the name *Ginevra* being a dialect form, in the feminine, of the Italian word for juniper (*ginepro*). A pun of this kind would certainly have appealed to Leonardo. Second, and much more important, is the internal evidence. The portrait reveals Leonardo's incomparable technical skill. There are passages, such as the modeling of the lips, which Leonardo never surpassed in delicacy. Such value transitions are miracles of technique, and Leonardo was the first painter to have the perfect control of his medium necessary to make light and shade merge imperceptibly.

In his notebooks, Leonardo compares curls of hair to swirling water. The ringlets which frame Ginevra's face resemble cascading whirlpools. These curls are so like Leonardo's rendering both of hair in his other paintings and of water in his drawings as to be a virtual signature. Lastly, there are Leonardo's colored reflections, discussed at length in his *Treatise on Painting*. In Ginevra's portrait such reflected colors reverberate through the painting and cause the flesh to glow as if, like the moon, it reflected some hidden radiance.

But we still have not answered the question of why the portrait is of such significance. The answer is that this is the first psychological portrait ever painted. Leonardo's tremendous innovation was developed in his three portraits of women. Each expresses a different mood: the earliest, *Ginevra*, withdrawn sadness; the next, *Cecilia Gallerani*, now in Krakow, appealing wistfulness; and the last, the *Mona Lisa*, mirthless amusement. Of these, the most original is the enigmatic melancholy of Ginevra de' Benci. Sadness has rarely been represented in portraiture. I know of no other instance in painting before the seventeenth century, and even then the tragic view of life was usually conveyed by portraits of men, not of women.

Collections: Possibly Niccolini and Benci families; possibly Prince Carl Eusebius of Liechtenstein; The Princes of Liechtenstein from 1733. *Ailsa Mellon Bruce Fund*, 1967. Painted c. 1480. Wood, 15⅛ × 14½" (38.2 × 36.7 cm.).

Jan van Eyck

(FLEMISH, 1380/1400-1441)

7   THE ANNUNCIATION

In many ways the founder of all Northern painting was Jan van Eyck, who died in Bruges in 1441. He is traditionally considered the discoverer of oil painting, a technique in which linseed oil serves as the solvent for pigment, rather than egg, which was used in the Italian technique of tempera. This made possible a new flexibility and delicacy of handling.

Whether or not van Eyck actually did discover oil painting may be debated, but certainly he was the first to achieve a naturalistic rendering of interior space, or in less technical terms, the effect of looking through an open window or door into a room. It is this new power of representation which is van Eyck's most salient characteristic. Note his masterful suggestion of atmosphere through subtle gradations of light, and his supreme skill in the definition of detail. Contrast the barely visible frescoes at the top of the dimly lit walls of the church, painted with an impalpable delicacy, and the hard microscopic clarity of the jewels on the angel's robes. No artist has ever had a greater range of visual effects. *The Annunciation*, however, is more than a record of new technical attainment; it is a masterpiece of Christian symbolism. It expounds the significance of the Annunciation, the momentous event in history which divides the Era of Law from the Era of Grace, the Dispensation of the Old Testament from the New. The dark upper part of the church with its single window on which is depicted Jehovah, the Lord of the Old Testament, is contrasted with the lower half illumined by three windows, symbolic of the Trinity, through which shines the Light of the World. The angel addresses Our Lady with the words *Ave Gratia Plena*, to which She answers *Ecce Ancilla Domini*, the words reversed and inverted so they can be read by the Holy Ghost, descending in rays of light.

The building cannot be identified with an existing church, but it suggests the late Romanesque style of Maastricht and Tournai. It would seem as though van Eyck designed this building in an architectural style which had not been practiced for several centuries, perhaps the first example of "revivalism" in architecture.

Collections: Thought to have been ordered by Philip the Good, Duke of Burgundy, for a church in Dijon; William II, King of the Netherlands; Hermitage Gallery, Leningrad. *Andrew W. Mellon Collection*, 1937. Painted c. 1425/30. Transferred from wood to canvas, 36½ x 14⅜" (93 x 36.5 cm.).

Petrus Christus

(FLEMISH, c. 1410–1472/73)

8   THE NATIVITY

Glimpses of landscape in Flemish painting are always rewarding. The background of the Petrus Christus *Nativity* shows how pleasant the countryside must have been in the fifteenth century. The town walls kept building within bounds. There were no suburbs. One stepped from the gate of the city directly into meadowland. Nothing could seem closer to an earthly paradise than the world the Flemish artists portrayed. Fortunately, the smells, the dirt, the lack of sanitation of urban life in the Middle Ages had no place in the visual arts.

Painters were not paid to represent the facts of life. Theirs was a different task—to portray the facts of religion. In the foreground of his painting Petrus Christus tells us the story of Man's Fall and Redemption; Adam and Eve stand on columns supported on the backs of stooped figures, symbolizing mankind burdened with Original Sin. Above on the arch are scenes showing the Expulsion from Eden, Cain slaying Abel, and other episodes from the Old Testament. In the spandrels are two battling figures, mankind in hopeless conflict and enmity as a consequence of sin.

These simulated sculpture groups provide the historical antecedents for the action in the center, where Mary and Joseph, accompanied by angels, worship the Redeemer. This moment of dramatic stillness, so portentous for mankind, must often have been acted out in a similar way in mystery plays, even to the wooden shoes of Joseph, which lend a sense of actuality to the scene. In the middle distance are four spectators, symbols of humanity, for whose Redemption the Incarnation has taken place. Confronted by a vision of compelling eloquence their indifference, so characteristic of mankind, remains tragically unchanged.

Collections: Prince Manuel Yturbe, Madrid; Duchess of Parcent, Madrid. *Andrew W. Mellon Collection*, 1937. Painted c. 1445. Wood, 51¼ × 38¼" (130 × 97 cm.).

Rogier van der Weyden

(FLEMISH, 1399/1400–1464)

9 PORTRAIT OF A LADY

Among the hundreds of portraits at the National Gallery of Art there is one as beautiful as it is baffling. It is the portrait by Rogier van der Weyden of a young lady tentatively identified as a famous heiress of the fifteenth century, Marie de Valengin, daughter of Philip the Good, Duke of Burgundy. The painting's attraction is twofold: its excellent preservation and the fascination of the lady who sat for it. As is usual with Flemish pictures of this period, it is painted on a piece of wood overlaid with white gesso. On this prepared panel the figure was first painted in monochrome, and the underpainting then covered with thin glazes of colored oil. With this newly discovered oil technique the artist was able to render the most subtle gradations of light, especially noticeable in passages such as the transparent wimple. With age such Flemish panels have acquired a web of minute cracks, a surface as beautiful in its way as the surface of old porcelain.

Although the precision of Flemish painting was suited to the firm structure and sharp contours of Marie de Valengin's features, if the sitter is she, the clarity of this style only stresses her somewhat eccentric appearance. She is too thin, her lips too thick, her forehead too high. Her looks are outré, defensible only on the basis of Sir Francis Bacon's axiom, "There is no excellent beauty that hath not some strangeness in the proportion." But ugly as her features may be individually, still they combine to suggest a personality so enigmatic, with so many conflicting tendencies, that one becomes absorbed and ends by finding Rogier van der Weyden's model not only enthralling but, in some way, strangely beautiful.

The first impression is of her preoccupation. Her stare, so oblivious of the spectator, is like a challenging withdrawal; she looks out from a citadel of secrecy. Then one notices her meager body made to appear still thinner by her silken girdle, and afterward her high, intellectual forehead, its domelike appearance exaggerated by its diaphanous covering. All this is psychologically consistent, every detail indicative of a contemplative, somewhat ascetic nature. But this is only one aspect of her character. There is another side, eagerly sensuous and fiercely passionate. It is shown by the thick underlip and the full mouth. Thus the actions of this Burgundian princess must always have been unpredictable, always determined by an unresolved conflict in her personality. She remains an enigma, with something of the perplexing quality of that Gothic lady whom John Skelton paradoxically describes:

> As midsummer flower
> Gentle as falcon
> Or hawk of the tower.

Collections: Duke of Anhalt-Dessau, Gotisches Haus, Wörlitz, and Herzogliches Schloss, Dessau, Germany. *Andrew W. Mellon Collection*, 1937. Painted c. 1455. Wood, 14½ x 10¾" (37 x 27 cm.).

Gerard David

(FLEMISH, c. 1460–1523)

10   THE REST ON THE FLIGHT INTO EGYPT

Flemish painting is characterized by a curious mixture of observation and tradition. In this connection the small wicker basket in the foreground of David's *Rest on the Flight into Egypt* is revealing. It is only natural that Our Lady should have taken a traveling bag on her journey, and for this accessory David designed a little reticule which was to prove so popular that it appears sporadically in other paintings for almost a hundred years. The scene depicted, a pause on a journey, is one he must often have seen. In the middle distance, the father, beating chestnuts from a tree, is gathering food, while in the foreground the mother has already begun to feed her child. But there is more in this scene than a glimpse of a family at mealtime. A transcript of actuality is combined with an ancient symbolism. A family pauses to eat, but the food, the grapes, are a sign of the Eucharist, a prefiguration of the Last Supper and of the suffering which awaits Our Lord. Early Flemish painting has often a double significance: as a mirror of everyday life and as a symbol of the life to come.

The popularity of David's painting is attested by the many existing copies and altered replicas. Possibly its charm for contemporaries lay in the originality of its coloring. The misty landscape, illumined with an azure light so characteristic of the Belgian countryside, echoes the color of the sky and of the Virgin's mantle. Four hundred years later Whistler might have entitled such a painting *A Symphony in Blue*. Is it perhaps the earliest tonal symphony with a dominant color in the history of art?

Collections: Rev. Montague Taylor, London; Rodolph Kann, Paris; J. Pierpont Morgan, New York. *Andrew W. Mellon Collection*, 1937. Painted c. 1510. Wood, 17¾ x 17½" (45 x 44.5 cm.).

Mathis Grünewald

(GERMAN, c. 1465–1528)

11   THE SMALL CRUCIFIXION

Heir to the Gothic and precursor of the Baroque, Grünewald has in this painting attained an unsurpassed intensity of expression. The hands and feet of Christ stab at one's heart. Twisted and tortured, they are visual symbols of physical agony. His torso, "dark smirched with pain," is drawn in by a paroxysm of suffering. John and the two Marys show their anguish with gestures prayerful but helpless. The mood of ineffable woe is enhanced by the dark gloom of night, and by the colors: murky greens, livid blues, and blood reds.

The Small Crucifixion is one of scarcely more than a dozen paintings by Grünewald, whose most famous picture is the great *Isenheim Altarpiece* at Colmar. It was known to Sandrart, who saw the panel in the possession of Duke Maximilian I of Bavaria. It had previously been owned, Sandrart tells us, by Maximilian's father, Duke William V of Bavaria, an "intelligent judge and connoisseur of fine art." Sandrart writes of it as follows: "[Duke William] had a small Crucifixion with Our Dear Lady and St. John, together with a kneeling and devoutly praying Mary Magdalen, most carefully painted by his [Grünewald's] hand, and he [the Duke] loved it very much, even without knowing whom it was by. On account of the wonderful Christ on the Cross, so suspended and supported on the feet, it is so very rare that real life could not surpass it and certainly it is more true to nature and reality than all Crucifixions when one contemplates it with thoughtful patience for a long time. For this reason it was, on the gracious order of the honorable Duke, engraved, half a sheet large, on copper in the year 1605 by Raphael Sadeler, and I pleased His Highness, the Great Elector Maximilian, of blessed memory, greatly since I made known the master's name." It is a name that has fascinated art historians ever since. A list made thirty years ago of the most significant publications on Mathis Grünewald since 1914 listed 436 books and articles.

Collections: Probably the Collegiate Church (*Stift*) of Aschaffenburg; Duke William V of Bavaria; Duke Maximilian I of Bavaria; Landrat Dr. Friedrich Schöne, Essen; Franz Wilhelm Koenigs and heirs, Haarlem. *Samuel H. Kress Collection*, 1961. Painted c. 1510. Wood, 24¼ x 18⅛" (61.6 x 46 cm.).

Albrecht Dürer

(GERMAN, 1471–1528)

12   PORTRAIT OF A CLERGYMAN

This famous portrait from the Czernin Collection, Vienna, is signed with Dürer's monogram and dated 1516. Though the subject has not been identified, the portrait is a brilliant example of Dürer's ability to "lay open the fine net-work of the heart and brain of man," to make us see deep into the soul until we understand, for example, the character of this ugly, resolute individual, whose personality, flashing out through luminous and asymmetrical eyes, exerts a powerful spell. His is the face of the Reformation. Here one sees that burning fanaticism which, occurring on both sides, caused the religious wars and, after a deluge of blood and destruction, left northern Europe bleak and desolate.

Dürer was not only capable of suggesting in his portraits the universal in the individual, he was also able to give a remarkable record of physical appearance. Trained by his work as an engraver and designer of woodcuts, he drew every form with the utmost precision. A trick of verisimilitude he often employed, until it became almost a signature, was to delineate the windowpanes of his studio as though reflected in the pupils of his sitter's eyes.

The technique of this painting is unusual: it is executed on parchment. Artists were constantly seeking new methods and materials, and in 1516 Dürer twice tried the skin of a goat or sheep as a support for his painting. Though the experiment apparently did not satisfy him, this portrait has lasted without a blemish, and one wonders why he abandoned an interesting innovation.

Collections: Paul von Praun, Nuremberg; Count Johann Rudolf Czernin von Chudenitz, Vienna; Czernin Gallery, Vienna. *Samuel H. Kress Collection*, 1952. Signed with monogram, and dated 1516. Parchment on canvas, 16⅞ x 13" (42.9 x 33.2 cm.).

Hans Holbein the Younger

(GERMAN, 1497-1543)

13 EDWARD VI AS A CHILD

As Hazlitt said, Holbein's portraits are like state documents. In them we find recorded objectively, but with impressive dignity, the figures who surrounded Henry VIII. This panel of Edward VI, painted soon after Holbein's second arrival in England, was given to Henry VIII on New Year's Day, 1539. It is listed in the Royal Inventory as "By Hanse Holbyne a table of the pictour of the p'nce [Prince's] grace." The King was undoubtedly pleased with the likeness, for according to the same document, he gave "To Hanse Holbyne, paynter, a gilte cruse [a type of cup] wt a cover Cornelis weing X oz. quarter."

The poem at the bottom of the picture was written by Cardinal Morison, an influential figure of the Church and Court. It urges Edward to emulate his illustrious father in every way, presumably in matrimony as in other matters. Healthy as the young Prince seems in this portrait, fate did not give him time to marry even once, for he died at the age of fifteen.

The English were easily pleased in matters of art. Since the monkish illuminators of the Middle Ages they had never produced or imported a painter of the first rank. Therefore when Holbein arrived from Switzerland his popularity was enormous. He was particularly admired for his ability to ennoble his sitters. Here, commissioned to paint a portrait of a child not yet two years old, he manages to convey rank and majesty. The future monarch of England is dressed in courtly clothes of gold and velvet; he holds his rattle as though it were a scepter, and he raises his right hand in a gesture of royal magnanimity. Thus an effigy becomes a symbol rather than a portrait. Holbein has presented the quintessence of royalty, the embodiment of the princely infant.

Collections: English Royal Collection; Arundel (where engraved in 1650); Provincial Museum, Hanover (from the Royal and Ducal Hanoverian Collections). *Andrew W. Mellon Collection*, 1937. Painted presumably in 1538. Wood, 22⅜ x 17⅜" (57 x 44 cm.).

PARVVLE PATRISSA, PATRIÆ VIRTVTIS ET HÆRES
   ESTO, NIHIL MAIVS MAXIMVS ORBIS HABET.
GNATVM VIX POSSVNT COELVM ET NATVRA DEDISSE,
   HVIVS QVEM PATRIS, VICTVS HONORET HONOS.
ÆQVATO TANTVM, TANTI TV FACTA PARENTIS,
   VOTA HOMINVM, VIX QVO PROGREDIANTVR, HABENT
VINCITO, VICISTI. QVOT REGES PRISCVS ADORAT
   ORBIS, NEC TE QVI VINCERE POSSIT, ERIT.   Ricard. Morysin. Car...

14

15

Lucas Cranach the Elder was one of the three greatest German painters, the other two being Dürer and Grünewald. The seven panels by Cranach in the National Gallery's collection are evidence of his ability as a portraitist, religious painter, and delineator of seductive nudes. His portraits and devotional pictures, however, have never been as popular with collectors as his enticing nymphs and naked goddesses. He was Hermann Goering's favorite artist, and the field marshall managed to loot a large number of Cranach nudes from all over Europe.

16

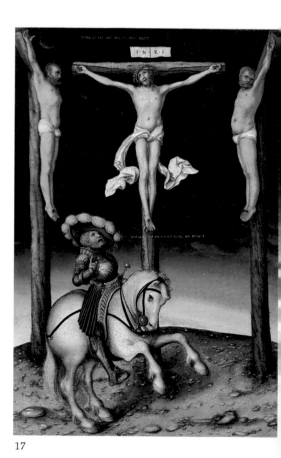

17

Lucas Cranach the Elder (German, 1472–1553)

14 *Portrait of a Man.* Dated 1522. Wood, 22⅜ x 15⅛" (56.8 x 38.4 cm.). Samuel H. Kress Collection

15 *Portrait of a Woman.* 1522. Wood, 22⅜ x 15" (56.8 x 38.1 cm.). Samuel H. Kress Collection

16 *A Princess of Saxony.* c. 1517. Wood, 17⅛ x 13½" (43.6 x 34.3 cm.). Ralph and Mary Booth Collection

17 *The Crucifixion with Longinus.* Dated 1536. Wood, 20 x 13¾" (50.8 x 34.9 cm.). Samuel H. Kress Collection

18 *Madonna and Child.* Probably c. 1535. Wood, 28 x 20½" (71.1 x 52.1 cm.). Gift of Adolph Caspar Miller

19 *The Nymph of the Spring.* After 1537. Wood, 19 x 28⅝" (48.5 x 72.9 cm.). Gift of Clarence Y. Palitz

18

19

Raphael

(UMBRIAN, 1483-1520)

20 ST. GEORGE AND THE DRAGON

Raphael was twenty-two or twenty-three when he painted *St. George and the Dragon*. He had already become one of the most accomplished masters in Italy. No painting reveals more clearly his serenity, his effortless achievement. But there has been a reaction against "the very rightness of Raphael's perfection." Appreciation has shifted. The lofty pinnacles of art are today often considered boring, and critics prefer to study the arduous ascent to these heights, to trace the tortuous route leading from the incompetent to the proficient. Thus the romantic basis of contemporary aesthetics has blinded many people to the beauty of Raphael's paintings.

This point of view, the exaltation of the half-realized, the half-expressed, accords with the art of our time. Modern painters lack the very qualities for which Raphael was preeminent. For more than a century painters have brought to their craft less and less of that easy fluency of draftsmanship, that simple felicity of composition, which Raphael took for granted. We have come to despise facility largely because facility of a high order has almost ceased to exist. Drawn by instinctive sympathy to contemporary art, many people, especially painters, have come to look on Raphael's work with prejudice. But his great paintings, such as the picture reproduced, should not be judged by the standards prevalent today. They should be judged by the standards which Sir Joshua Reynolds termed "the great style," and which in Italy is termed the *gusto grande* and in France the *beau idéal*. For these are the terms of excellence which people of culture have accepted for over four hundred years. If we use them as a measure of Raphael's achievement, we shall find that he has given us a supreme expression of the classical style.

Collections: Commissioned by Duke Guidobaldo da Montefeltro, the ruler of Urbino, and taken as a gift to Henry VII of England by Count Baldassare Castiglione; Third Earl of Pembroke (engraved by L. Vorsterman in 1627); Fourth Earl of Pembroke gave it to Charles I of England in exchange for the Holbein drawings now at Windsor Castle; Charles d'Escoubleau, Marquis de Sourdis, Paris; Laurent de Tessier de Montarsy; Pierre Crozat; Louis-François Crozat, Marquis de Châtel; Louis-Antoine Crozat, Baron de Thiers; Catherine II, Empress of Russia; Hermitage Gallery, Leningrad. *Andrew W. Mellon Collection*, 1937. Signed. Painted 1504/6. Wood, 11⅛ x 8⅜" (28.5 x 21.5 cm.).

Raphael

(UMBRIAN, 1483-1520)

21 THE ALBA MADONNA

The Alba Madonna was painted about 1510, after Raphael had arrived in Rome and had fallen under the spell of Michelangelo. It is one of the supreme compositional achievements of Renaissance painting, for balance in a tondo, or round picture, required the utmost delicacy in adjustment. If the masses are not in equilibrium, the picture will seem to roll like a wheel. In the *Alba Madonna* this complex problem is solved and the result is one of extraordinary stability. The compact group of figures in the foreground is also related to the surrounding landscape, with that feeling for perfect spatial composition which was Raphael's greatest achievement.

The picture was taken to Spain at the end of the seventeenth century by the Spanish viceroy in Naples, Don Gaspar de Guzmán; shortly thereafter it entered the collection of the Duchess of Alba, where it remained for more than a hundred years, thus acquiring its present name. Powerful as the Albas were, they were nonetheless forced by Charles IV to allow Manuel Godoy to buy the picture for his palace of Buenavista, even though it was entailed in their estates. A handsome profligate, Godoy depended for his power on the infatuation of the Queen and the curious complaisance of her cuckold husband. Married to the King's niece (whose portrait by Goya is shown in plate 63), Godoy became prime minister and virtual ruler. But he was so inept, first opposing the leaders of the French Revolution and then toadying to them, that when Napoleon's armies moved into Spain, he was arrested by the Prince of the Asturias, the King's eldest son, who controlled the government for a short time. Godoy's collection was immediately confiscated and put up for sale. The Albas tried through a lawsuit to recover their *Madonna*, but failed. Instead, the Danish Ambassador in Madrid, Count de Bourke, bought it, took it to London, and sold it at auction for £4,000 to W. G. Coesvelt—a thousand pounds less than the painter and art dealer Johann Zoffany had asked for Raphael's *The Niccolini-Cowper Madonna* a quarter-century earlier. Prices were rising, however, and Coesvelt made a handsome profit a few years later when he sold *The Alba Madonna* to the Curator of the Hermitage Gallery for £14,000. The Russians in turn waited a hundred years and sold the picture to Andrew Mellon for £233,000. Even though somewhat out of fashion today, Raphael's paintings have continued to rise in price, and his Madonnas are still the soundest of investments.

Collections: Church of Monteoliveto, Nocera di Pagani, near Naples; Don Gaspar Méndez de Haro y Guzmán, Naples; the Dukes of Alba, Madrid; Don Manuel Godoy, Principe de la Paz; Count Edmond de Bourke, Danish Ambassador to Spain; W. G. Coesvelt, London; Hermitage Gallery, Leningrad. *Andrew W. Mellon Collection*, 1937. Painted c. 1510. Transferred from wood to canvas, diameter 37¼" (94.5 cm.).

Giorgione

(VENETIAN, c. 1478–1510)

22 THE ADORATION OF THE SHEPHERDS

What we have come to call the Giorgionesque was as revolutionary in the Renaissance as was Cubism at the beginning of the twentieth century. In the early Renaissance, paintings were thought of as colored drawings modeled in light and shade to suggest relief. Later artists observed that we do not normally see the separate contours of objects but that their forms seem to melt into each other and to fuse with the surrounding atmosphere. The crystalline clarity of early morning, which is characteristic of the fifteenth century and can be seen in the Botticelli *Adoration* (plate 5), changes in the new style to the misty sunlight of late afternoon. This soft illumination increases unity of effect. Giorgione, who died in 1510, presumably at the age of thirty-two, has been credited with these innovations, which found their fullest development among Venetian painters. But actually the Giorgionesque, like Cubism, was a way of painting adopted simultaneously by a number of artists. *The Adoration of the Shepherds*, for example, has been attributed in turn to the three leading painters of Venice at the beginning of the sixteenth century, Giorgione, Bellini, and Titian.

Today, an increasing number of experts believe the picture to be by Giorgione, and this is the attribution which most clearly describes its style. Bernard Berenson, the most famous of all critics of Italian art, remained adamant for many years in his opposition to ascribing this painting to Giorgione. Joseph Duveen, the art dealer who owned the picture at the time, tried in every way to make Berenson alter his opinion. This led to their celebrated quarrel. At the end of his life, however, Berenson did change his mind and concluded that the painting was at least in part by Giorgione, working in collaboration with Titian. Berenson's theory is borne out by X-rays which show a number of changes from the original composition. Similar alterations, but on a much greater scale, were made by Titian when he repainted Giovanni Bellini's *Feast of the Gods* (plate 23).

Collections: Cardinal Joseph Fesch, Rome; Claudius Tarral, Paris; Thomas Wentworth Beaumont, Bretton Hall, Yorkshire; Wentworth Blackett Beaumont, First Lord Allendale; the Viscounts Allendale, London. *Samuel H. Kress Collection*, 1939. Painted c. 1505/10. Wood, 35¾ x 43½" (91 x 111 cm.).

Giovanni Bellini

(VENETIAN, c. 1430–1516)

23   THE FEAST OF THE GODS

The connoisseurship of painting offers, from time to time, investigations as fascinating and complex as a detective story. *The Feast of the Gods*, for example, is signed by Giovanni Bellini. Yet Titian, according to Vasari, brought it to completion. A composite X-ray of the painting indicates that the picture has had three backgrounds. There is evidence that the final alterations, and perhaps the earlier changes as well, are due to Titian. As far as one can tell, his motives were mixed; but the impelling reason seems to have been that the original design did not harmonize with the other pictures in the same room in the Castle of Ferrara which Alfonso d'Este asked him to paint: *Bacchus and Ariadne*, now in London, and *The Venus Worship* and *The Andrians*, now in Madrid.

Although Titian finally transformed the background of *The Feast of the Gods* into a landscape which has been judged "the finest that up to that time had ever been painted . . . an epoch in the history of art," still, from the beginning, Bellini's painting was an astounding innovation. One remarkable feature is the representation of the gods and goddesses in the guise of everyday people. It is as though they had become players in a Renaissance masque. The scene they act out, a story told by Ovid, explains the annual sacrifice made by the Romans to Priapus. On the left the ass of Silenus brays and arouses the drowsy deities as, on the right, the god of fertility secretly approaches the goddess of chastity. Then, as Ovid says, "The nymph in terror started up . . . and flying gave the alarm to the whole grove; . . . the god in the moonlight was laughed at by all." However, at the touch of Bellini's brush the ribald joke undergoes a metamorphosis, becomes a noble Dionysiac mystery, much as Shakespeare's alchemy transmutes leaden stories into golden plays.

Collections: Duke Alfonso I d'Este, Ferrara; Cardinal Pietro Aldobrandini and family, Rome; Vincenzo Camuccini, Rome; Duke of Northumberland, Alnwick Castle, England. *Widener Collection*, 1942. Signed, and dated 1514. Canvas, 67 x 74" (170 x 188 cm.).

Titian

(VENETIAN, c. 1477–1576)

24 DOGE ANDREA GRITTI

The seal of Charles I of England and a label reading, "Bought for his Majesty in Italy, 1626," are still preserved on the back of the canvas of this stupendous portrait, more recently in the Czernin Collection in Vienna. The royal catalogue also listed it: "Duke Grettie, of Venice, with his right hand holding his robes. Bought by the King, half figures so big as the life, in a black wooden gilded frame." Perhaps Charles saw in the stern, implacable face of the Venetian Doge those traits of character he himself lacked. Titian has dowered Gritti with a grim, ruthless personality and made him a symbol of the power of the galleys that, under the patronage of St. Mark, caused Venice to be honored and feared along the trade routes of the world. But Gritti was also a patron of the arts. At his order, a considerable number of Titian's large religious, historical, and allegorical pictures, now mostly lost, were painted.

The hand with which the Doge grasps his flowing cape may be based upon the hand of Moses in the famous statue by Michelangelo in Rome. A Venetian sculptor, Jacopo Sansovino, is believed to have brought a cast of this hand to Venice, where Titian probably studied its massive power to help him create an image of uncompromising majesty, the archetype of the imperious ruler moving forward in a ceremonial procession.

Collections: King Charles I of England; Wenzel Anton, Prince von Kaunitz-Rietburg, Chancellor of Empress Maria Theresa; Count Johann Rudolf Czernin von Chudenitz, Vienna; Czernin Gallery, Vienna. *Samuel H. Kress Collection*, 1961. Signed. Painted probably between 1535 and 1540. Canvas, 52½ x 40⅝" (133.6 x 103.2 cm.).

45

Titian

(VENETIAN, c. 1477–1576)

25   VENUS WITH A MIRROR

Titian, more than any other Renaissance artist, understood the spirit of classical art. Yet he was nearly seventy when he went to Rome and had his first opportunity to visit the capital of the ancient world and to see the great works of art accumulated there. When he was not executing his many important missions at the Vatican and among the Roman nobility, he was, as he said, "learning from the marvelous, ancient stones." Although he regretted that he had not received this inspiration earlier, still it came at a time when he was about to enter upon his period of supreme achievement, which lasted until he was well into his nineties. Under the influence of classical art his late nudes gained an amplitude of form, a heavy magnificence which suggests Greek sculpture of the Golden Age.

From his earliest masterpieces like the Bacchanals, painted for the Duke of Ferrara, to canvases like this, painted when he was over seventy, Titian repeatedly celebrated the goddess of love. All these pictures are permeated with a sensuality which deepens with age, growing always more impersonal. In his final work he expresses the indwelling power of feminine beauty, a quality which transcends the loveliness of any individual woman. These pictures are his final homage to Venus, as moving in their way as the late love poems of Yeats.

But Titian's amatory tribute was not arrived at suddenly. From data revealed by recent X-rays it appears that the canvas was used previously for two other compositions, which Titian abandoned in succession. The first was a horizontal composition of a man and a woman standing together, possibly an allegory of marriage with the bride and groom in the roles of Venus and Mars. The second was a vertical composition representing a Venus with two cupids; the head and pose of the Venus were retained in the final picture.

Having found the composition he wanted, Titian painted several further variations on this theme, and still others were produced by followers and imitators, but this particular canvas he kept for himself, feeling for it perhaps some special affection. After his death it was sold by his son Pomponio to the Barbarigo family, and remained in their possession until it was purchased by Nicholas I for the Hermitage Gallery, Leningrad.

Collections: Pomponio Vecellio, Venice; Barbarigo family, Venice; Hermitage Gallery, Leningrad. *Andrew W. Mellon Collection*, 1937. Painted c. 1555. Canvas, 49 x 41½" (124.5 x 105.5 cm.).

François Clouet

(FRENCH, c. 1510-1572)

26 "DIANE DE POITIERS"

François Clouet's work is an example of the wide dissemination in the sixteenth century of the Italian style. This is one of three portraits he signed. In the nineteenth century the sitter was considered to be Diane de Poitiers, and the portrait retained this title for many years. The children in the painting were supposed to be the offspring of her lover Henri II and Catherine de' Medici. We know they were placed in her care. The unicorn embroidered on a chair back or firescreen was thought to be a reference to the unicorn horn purchased by Diane to preserve the health of the royal children through its supposed therapeutic properties.

More recently the date of the picture has been placed much later, toward the end of Clouet's life. The lady's coiffure, for example, resembles that of Clouet's portrait of Elizabeth of Austria, a drawing for which is dated 1571. As Diane died in 1566, scholars have gone in search of some other royal favorite. Gabrielle d'Estrées, mistress of Henri IV, and Marie Touchet, mistress of Charles IX, have had their advocates but have yet to gain general acceptance. In 1966 Roger Trinquet published the most fascinating suggestion of all. He believes the lady to be Mary Queen of Scots and the painting to have been done with satirical intent for some Huguenot patron, possibly François, Maréchal de Montmorency.

Although the lady's face is highly idealized, a beautiful feminine mask, there is no doubt that she resembles accepted portraits of the tragic Scottish queen, particularly a drawing in white mourning attire attributed to Francois Clouet. If this identification is correct, then the infant is her son and the crossed black bands on his swaddling clothes an allusion to the Cross of St. Andrew and possibly also to the death of Darnley, the baby's father. The same child at four or five would then be the boy reaching for the fruit, a symbol of his grasping for the crown of Scotland. There is also the supporting evidence that the unicorn and the grapes appear in emblematic devices of Mary Stuart; and Colin Eisler, who is inclined to accept this identification, has pointed out that the bather's cap "is closer to English than to French fashion."

The setting may seem unusual, but judging by the numerous copies of this picture in the sixteenth century and the variations on the theme of a lady in her bath, which continued into the seventeenth century, Clouet's painting made bathing portraits extremely fashionable.

Collections: Sir Richard Frederick, Burwood Park; Cook, Doughty House, Richmond, Surrey. *Samuel H. Kress Collection*, 1961. Painted probably c. 1571. Wood, 36¼ × 32" (92.1 × 81.3 cm.).

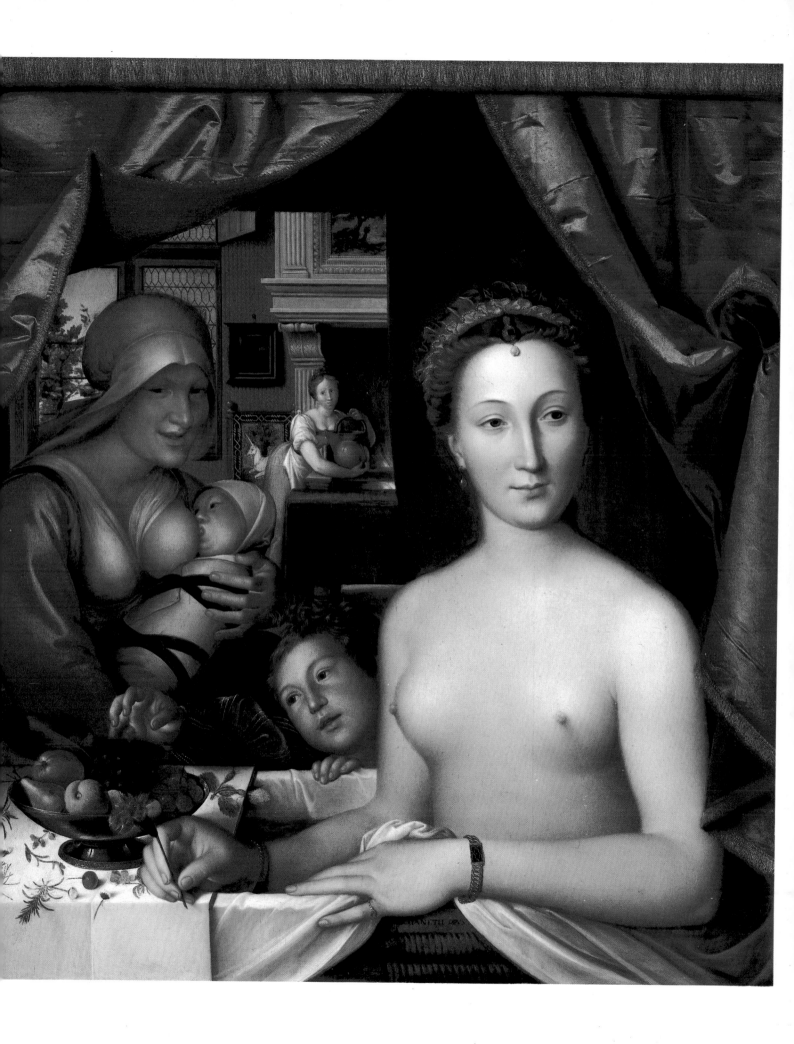

Jacopo Tintoretto

(VENETIAN, 1518–1594)

27 CHRIST AT THE SEA OF GALILEE

Ask a contemporary painter to name the greatest of the Venetian artists, and the chances are he will choose Tintoretto. There are many reasons for this choice, but in the painting reproduced one is especially evident: Tintoretto's emotional intensity. In *Christ at the Sea of Galilee*, the event illustrated is described in John 21:7. Our Lord, standing on the shore, reveals himself to his disciples who are fishing: "Now when Simon Peter heard that it was the Lord, he girt his fisher's coat unto him (for he was naked), and did cast himself into the sea." Here almost for the first time nature becomes an actor in the drama. The driven clouds, the storm-tossed waves, the "light that never was, on sea or land," all heighten the terrible intensity of the moment of ecstatic union when man is irresistibly drawn to His Lord and Saviour. How marvelously Tintoretto conveys the towering majesty of Christ and the yearning desire of the disciple who flings himself into the sea to reach his Master!

It is interesting to note that Hans Tietze, one of the most astute authorities on Venetian painting, always believed this picture to be by El Greco. The elongation of Christ, the color and modeling of the waves, and the emotional intensity of the scene suggest the Spanish painter. But it is hard to place the picture in the chronology of El Greco's works, and the touch in the smaller figures and the painting of the sky seem typical of Tintoretto's style.

Collections: Count J. Galotti; Arthur Sachs, New York. *Samuel H. Kress Collection*, 1952. Painted c. 1575/80. Canvas, 46 x 66¼" (117 x 168.5 cm.).

El Greco

(SPANISH, 1541-1614)

28 LAOCOÖN

Among the Old Masters, the true prophet of modern art is El Greco. His work foreshadows the abandonment three hundred years later of naturalism for Expressionism, of proportions determined by nature for proportions determined by emotion. Academic critics fighting this trend used to assert that El Greco distorted the human form because his eyesight was defective. We now believe that astigmatism affected him less, if at all, than the stylization of Byzantine icons and mosaics he had seen as a young man on his native island of Crete. But the vogue for tall, slender figures with small heads, which became modish in European painting of the late sixteenth century, also played its part and prepared the public to accept the exaggerated elongations El Greco found suitable for his highly emotional style.

Although El Greco was born a Greek (his name was Domenikos Theotokópoulos), he ignored the mythology and the history of his fatherland except for this one subject. In the inventory of his possessions made in 1614 three Laocoöns are listed, one of which is similar in measurements to the painting reproduced here. El Greco may have been working on this particular version when he died, for a recent cleaning suggests that the three figures on the right remained unfinished.

The story of Laocoön is told by Arctinus of Miletus and repeated with some variations by Vergil. Laocoön was a priest of Poseidon who warned his fellow Trojans not to carry into their city the wooden horse left behind by the invading Greeks. But his famous words, "Fools, trust not the Greeks, even when bearing gifts," went unheeded. In despair he hurled his spear against the horse, a gesture of sacrilege against Minerva, to whom the wooden statue had been dedicated. The deities, perhaps portrayed on the right of the canvas, avenged this desecration by causing sea serpents to kill Laocoön and his two sons. Their deaths were interpreted by the Trojans as a sign of the anger of the gods, and the horse was brought inside the city walls. At night Greek soldiers concealed inside its belly crept out and opened the city gates, thus bringing about the fall of Troy and ending the Trojan War. In the middle distance the wooden horse can be seen, and in place of Troy is a view of Toledo, El Greco's adopted home.

Collections: Probably the large painting of Laocoön listed in the inventory of El Greco's estate in Toledo; Duke of Montpensier, Palace of San Telmo, Seville; Infante Don Antonio d'Orléans, Sanlúcar de Barrameda; E. Fischer, Charlottenburg; Prince Paul of Yugoslavia, Belgrade. *Samuel H. Kress Collection,* 1946. Painted c. 1610. Canvas, 54⅛ x 67⅞" (137.5 x 172.5 cm.).

Diego Velázquez

(SPANISH, 1599–1660)

29   THE NEEDLEWOMAN

The few pictures Velázquez painted to please himself are among his finest and most original achievements. In such paintings as the two views of the garden of the Villa Medici in the Prado and *The Needlewoman* in the National Gallery of Art, he appears a precursor of Corot, revealing a similar simplicity of treatment joined to a penetrating power of observation.

It would seem at first as though this study of a woman sewing were never finished. The left hand is merely blocked in, and the fingers of the right barely indicated. But this device of adumbrating rather than defining shapes was used by Velázquez in a number of late works to suggest motion. In the painting of Innocent X in the Palazzo Doria in Rome the outlines of the fingers are blurred, an indistinction which makes them seem to twitch with nervous energy. Again there is the hand of the boy with his foot on the dog in *Las Meninas*, where a flickering movement is given by making the contours seem faltering or indiscernible; and in *Las Hilanderas* if one looks at the hand of the woman in the foreground one sees what appear to be successive positions of her fingers as she winds her yarn. In all these pictures the vibrating effect of shifting planes of light conveys a sense of motion in a way that is new in art. Similarly *The Needlewoman* may not be an incomplete work but rather an experiment on the road leading to Impressionism.

A. Mayer identifies the sitter with the painter's daughter Francisca, who married his pupil Juan Bautista del Mazo; and Sánchez Cantón suggests that this painting may be a *Head of a Woman Sewing* mentioned in the inventory of Velázquez' effects at the time of his death.

Collections: Amédée, Marquis de Gouvello de Keriaval, Château de Kerlevenant, Sarzeau, Morbihan, Brittany; Mme Christiane de Polès, Paris. *Andrew W. Mellon Collection*, 1937. Painted c. 1640. Canvas, 29⅛ x 23⅝" (74 x 60 cm.).

Bartolomé Esteban Murillo

(SPANISH, 1617–1682)

30   A GIRL AND HER DUENNA

All the paintings we have reproduced so far have been either devotional pictures, allegorical or mythological scenes, or portraits. In the seventeenth century scenes of daily life—genre subjects—came into fashion. In the past such material was to be found with rare exception only in the cheaper media of woodcut and engraving. This double portrait is essentially a genre picture. A young girl and her duenna stare boldly at the spectator, much as Murillo must have seen such women gazing from the high windows in the narrow streets of Seville. The painting was popularly known as *Las Gallegas*, the Galicians, referring to the tradition that it represents two notorious courtesans of Seville who originally came from the province of Galicia. Murillo was an artist of the people: genial, commonplace in outlook, with an easy eloquence. In religious painting his sentiment was torrential, and his immense popularity finally wore away a technical ability which was second only to that of Velázquez. Disconcertingly uneven as was his achievement, he occasionally created a masterpiece like the present picture. Here he has avoided the sticky sentimentality and trite picturesqueness which spoil so much of his work. He presents these two women with that detached observation which is the hallmark of the best Spanish painting.

What Northern artist would have treated the subject with such subtle restraint? Rembrandt alone would have had the insight to eliminate the extraneous and focus attention, as Murillo has done, on the young girl so beautifully placed in the window, so plastically rendered. But not even Frans Hals would have had sufficient alertness of vision to suggest the smile of the older woman, witty, sardonic, yet expressed by the eyes and cheek alone.

Collections: Duque de Almodóvar, Madrid; Lord Heytesbury, Heytesbury House, Wiltshire. *Widener Collection*, 1942. Painted c. 1670. Canvas, 50¼ x 41¾" (127.7 x 106.1 cm.).

Peter Paul Rubens

(FLEMISH, 1577–1640)

31 DEBORAH KIP, WIFE OF SIR BALTHASAR GERBIER, AND HER CHILDREN

The mood of introspection of the Gerbier family is puzzling, particularly as it is virtually unique in Rubens' work. Why does Lady Gerbier appear so withdrawn, as though meditating on some inner problem, which her elder son, looking at her almost beseechingly, seems to share? The two daughters gaze appraisingly and joylessly at the spectator. Only the baby is unaffected by this atmosphere of somber contemplation, which somehow suggests unhappiness, an air of foreboding.

How easy it is to invent the psychology of others, especially in paintings! There is nonetheless in this case reason to believe that Lady Gerbier had many problems which might well have made her pensive, if not melancholy. She was married to a scoundrel, and perhaps Rubens saw reflected in her face the tragedies —debts, frauds, even murder—which were to plague her life.

We can identify these sitters because the group portrait in the National Gallery of Art has been repeated on a much larger canvas, with the additions of Gerbier, five more children, and a coat of arms. George Vertue knew both pictures and discussed them in his unpublished letters in the British Museum. In 1749 he was asked to examine a sketch, sent from Flanders, of a painting offered to the Prince of Wales purporting to be a portrait of Sir Balthazar Arundel and his family. Vertue soon established that no one of that name had ever existed. Nevertheless the picture was bought for the Prince, and Vertue was called in again. In examining the purchase he found a half-erased inscription, "La Famille de Balthasar Gerbiere Chevaliere," and he identified the Gerbier coat of arms. The Prince was shocked. "How shall I come off of this?" he said to Vertue, "I have for this month past told many persons of quality that I have purchased a family peece of the Sheffield ancestor to the late Duke of Buckingham . . . as I was assured it (was) . . . be said the truth that dealers in pictures are like false moneyers." The picture the "false moneyers" sold the Prince is now in the Rubens Room at Windsor Castle, labeled correctly *Sir Balthazar Gerbier and His Family*. It is a rather poor copy in its central part of the National Gallery of Art painting. The latter, according to Vertue, "was sold at Lord Radnor's in St. James Square, there I saw Lord Burlington bid five hundred pounds for it, and Mr. Scowen bought it. . . . many years afterwards Mr. Scowen being obliged to sell it . . . it was bot by a Gent of the Law, who lately sold it to Mr. Gideon, the Jew." One of Gideon's descendants married into the Fremantle family, and the painting was owned by the family until it was acquired by the National Gallery.

Collections: Balthazar Gerbier; First Earl of Radnor; Thomas Scowen; Sampson Gideon and descendants; Baron Eardley; Sir Culling Eardley; Mrs. W. H. Fremantle; Colonel F. E. Fremantle; E. V. Fremantle, Esq., Belvedere, Kent. *Andrew W. Mellon Fund, 1971.* Painted 1629–30. Canvas, 64¼ x 70" (165.8 x 177.8 cm.).

Sir Anthony van Dyck

(FLEMISH, 1599-1641)

32 MARCHESA ELENA GRIMALDI,
WIFE OF MARCHESE NICOLA CATTANEO

Paintings have their vicissitudes, as do human beings. Van Dyck's portrait of the Marchesa Elena Grimaldi has experienced the mutability of fortune. It was probably painted in 1623, when the artist was a young man, still at the height of his vigor. He had left his native Flanders and settled temporarily in Genoa, where he became overnight the fashionable portraitist of the patrician families. There he created on canvas a race of supermen and superwomen, richly dressed, of lofty stature and aloof expression. However, of all the Genoese who sat for him, van Dyck has given to none so dignified, so majestic a pose as to the wife of the Marchese Cattaneo. He has also favored her with perhaps his most brilliant design. How skillfully the parasol is used to heighten still further the Marchesa's tallness, "towering in her pride of place" as she advances across her terrace and casts at the spectator, far below, an appraising glance! This is the ultimate in the grand manner in portraiture.

The failure of their trade and the decline of their independence, however, brought the great families of Genoa close to destitution. English collectors cast covetous eyes on their works of art, and especially on the Marchesa Grimaldi's portrait. Sir David Wilkie in 1828 wrote Sir Robert Peel saying he had heard from his agent that in the palace of Nicola Cattaneo there was a picture of "a Young Lady, with a Black Servant holding a Curious Parasol over her head," which he tried to buy. The family would not sell, but should he try once more? Apparently the later efforts of Wilkie's agent were equally unavailing, for early in this century, when the van Dyck scholar Lionel Cust gained admission to the Cattaneo palace, he was ushered into a room where he halted spellbound. "From every wall, as it seemed, Van Dyck looked down, and on one there stood and gazed at me a haughty dame, over whose head a negro-page held a scarlet parasol. All, however, spoke of dust and neglect, and when I left the palace, it was with a feeling of regret that such treasures of painting should be left to moulder on the walls." Van Dyck's masterworks were not to crumble away much longer; they had in fact reached the nadir of their fortune. A dealer bought all the Cattaneo paintings shortly before World War I, and eventually P. A. B. Widener acquired the most important of the lot, the portrait of the Marchesa Grimaldi and the portraits of her two children (overleaf). These he gave with the rest of his collection to the nation.

Collection: Palazzo Cattaneo, Genoa. *Widener Collection*, 1942. Painted probably 1623. Canvas, 97 x 68" (246 x 173 cm.).

33

34

35

As a rough generalization van Dyck can be said to have had four periods: his education in Rubens' workshop, c. 1617; his Italian period, spent mostly at Genoa, 1621–27; his second Flemish period, 1628–32; and his English period, 1632 until his death in 1641. The paintings shown here belong to van Dyck's Genoese period. This is generally considered his most creative time. He was in full possession of his immense talent, and, eager to win renown, he poured all his genius into portraying the Genoese nobility.

There are sixteen portraits by van Dyck in the collection of the National Gallery of Art. Nowhere in the world can his work be studied more thoroughly. His fame had become so prodigious that he was overwhelmed with commissions; and he relied greatly on well-trained assistants who worked in his studio in England.

36

37

Sir Anthony van Dyck (Flemish, 1599–1641)

33 *Paola Adorno, Marchesa Brignole Sale, and Her Son.* c. 1625. Canvas, 74½ x 55″ (189.2 x 139.7 cm.). Widener Collection

34 *Clelia Cattaneo, Daughter of Marchesa Elena Grimaldi.* Dated 1623. Canvas, 48⅛ x 33⅛″ (122.3 x 84.2 cm.). Widener Collection

35 *Filippo Cattaneo, Son of Marchesa Elena Grimaldi.* Dated 1623. Canvas, 48⅛ x 33⅛″ (122.3 x 84.2 cm.). Widener Collection

36 *Giovanni Vincenzo Imperiale.* Dated 1625. Canvas, 50 x 41½″ (127 x 105.5 cm.). Widener Collection

37 *Marchesa Balbi.* 1622/27. Canvas, 72 x 48″ (183 x 122 cm.). Andrew W. Mellon Collection

38 *The Prefect Raphael Racius.* c. 1625. Canvas, 51⅝ x 41⅝″ (131 x 105.5 cm.). Widener Collection

38

Frans Hals

(DUTCH, c. 1580–1666)

39 BALTHASAR COYMANS

Frans Hals is an artist difficult to evaluate. Although it can be said that there is more truth in one of his portraits than in a gallery of portraits by van Dyck, this truth is superficial. We know this young Coymans as we might know someone on shipboard who passes our deck chairs daily but whom we never meet. Was he really as jaunty as all that? Was he proud of his coat of arms, which enables us to identify his family (*koey* means "cow" therefore, *koeymans*, "the cowman")? What was he really like?

The painting is dated 1645, and it has recently been pointed out that the inscription originally gave the sitter's age as 22 (the second digit has since been clumsily altered to a 6). If the subject of the portrait was only twenty-two in 1645, he may well have been not Balthasar, who was born in 1618, but Balthasar's cousin Willem Coymans, born in 1623. Whichever young man is represented, he was the scion of a distinguished and prosperous family. Yet Hals has stressed not his wealth and position but his youth and high spirits, and with the tilt of a hat has given him the appearance of a common rake. Was Hals after all an inverted alchemist, transmuting the gold we all believe exists in our personality into its true lead? And was van Dyck the true alchemist, giving his sitters something of the sublimity they sensed in themselves? As Fromentin wrote, van Dyck was "admired everywhere, welcomed everywhere . . . the equal of the greatest lords, the favorite and the friend of kings," whereas Frans Hals died in the poorhouse. Few sitters want truth in portraiture, even a superficial truth.

Van Dyck could flatter and he was an able painter, but he was not a virtuoso like Hals. The pyrotechnics of Hals' brush remain unique. With what genius he controls its swordplay! How far he soars above his disciples, artists like Sargent and Duveneck! Those of us who love painting for its own sake will find more delight in the sleeve and collar of Coymans' shirt than in all the paint-ennobled aristocracy of Sir Anthony van Dyck.

Collections: Coymans family, Haarlem; Mrs. Frederick Wollaston, London; Rodolphe Kann, Paris; Mrs. Collis P. Huntington, New York; Archer E. Huntington, New York. *Andrew W. Mellon Collection*, 1937. Dated 1645. Canvas, 30¼ x 25" (77 x 64 cm.).

Frans Hals (Dutch, c. 1580–1666)

40   *Portrait of an Elderly Lady.* Dated 1633. Canvas, 40¼ x 34″ (103 x 86.4 cm.). Andrew W. Mellon Collection

41   *Portrait of an Officer.* c. 1640. Canvas, 33¾ x 27″ (86 x 69 cm.). Andrew W. Mellon Collection

42   *Portrait of a Young Man.* c. 1645. Canvas, 26⅞ x 21⅞″ (68 x 56 cm.). Andrew W. Mellon Collection

43   *Portrait of a Man.* c. 1655/60. Canvas, 25 x 21″ (63.5 x 53.5 cm.). Widener Collection

44   *A Young Man in a Large Hat.* c. 1628/30. Canvas, 11½ x 9⅛″ (29 x 23 cm.). Andrew W. Mellon Collection

45   *Portrait of a Gentleman.* c. 1650/52. Canvas, 45 x 33½″ (114 x 85 cm.). Widener Collection

46   *Portrait of a Man.* c. 1650/52. Canvas, 37 x 29½″ (94 x 75 cm.). Andrew W. Mellon Collection

40

41

42

43

44

45

46

Frans Hals was one of the first artists in Europe to paint *alla prima* (i.e., directly on the canvas without preliminary underpainting). This rapid technique is the one normally used by modern painters. It is especially adapted to catching momentary expressions and gestures, as one can see in these reproductions. The comment about the superficiality of Hals' interpretation of his sitters in the discussion of *Balthasar Coymans* (plate 39) must be modified by saying that at the end of his life he showed a far deeper insight into character (see plate 45).

Rembrandt van Ryn

(DUTCH, 1606-1669)

47   SELF-PORTRAIT

Rembrandt was a much more profound artist than Frans Hals. Few autobiographies are as searching as his self-portraits. The one reproduced here was signed and dated 1659, ten years before his death. In 1656 he had been declared bankrupt and during the next two years everything he owned was sold. His son and his mistress were shortly to make themselves custodians even of his still-unpainted pictures. Once more he looked in a mirror to take stock of himself, to analyze the problem of his personality. He saw reflected a face lined with age and misfortune. He saw eyes which had searched more profoundly into the human soul than those of any other artist. He saw a mouth and a chin weak, infirm of purpose, manifesting that flaw in his character which had ruined his life. His hands are grasped as though in anguish at the spectacle of a self-ruined man. There exists no painting more pitiless in its analysis or more pitiful in its implications.

Collection: Duke of Buccleuch, London. *Andrew W. Mellon Collection*, 1937. Signed, and dated 1659. Canvas, 33¼ x 26″ (84 x 66 cm.).

Rembrandt van Ryn

(DUTCH, 1606–1669)

48   THE MILL

The Mill is Rembrandt's supreme achievement in landscape painting. It is usually dated about 1650, when he was still at the height of his fame. John Constable judged it "sufficient to form an epoch in the art . . . the first picture in which a sentiment has been expressed by chiaroscuro only, all details being excluded." And this melancholy sentiment, this mood of sublime sadness, which Rembrandt conveys through the stark simplicity of a windmill silhouetted in the fading light against the mist-filled sky, is indescribably moving. As Roger Fry has said, "It is surely the most complete expression of the dramatic mood in landscape that has ever been achieved in Western art."

Probably no single canvas has so strongly affected English painting. Turner admired it, and the notes in his sketchbook show that it was the basis of his conception of Rembrandt's handling of light. Sir Joshua Reynolds painted a free adaptation of it; and it was engraved by Charles Turner for his *Gems of Art*, a book to be found in the studio of nearly every nineteenth-century English painter.

In his autobiography, Peter Widener, the son and grandson of the founders of the collection, says that when Wilhelm von Bode, director of the Kaiser Friedrich Museum and an authority on Rembrandt, came to Lynnewood Hall to see the collection, he sat for half an hour contemplating *The Mill*. Finally he turned to Joseph Widener, who was waiting for his opinion, and said, "This is the greatest picture in the world. The greatest picture by any artist."

Collections: Duc d'Orléans, Paris; William Smith, London; Marquess of Lansdowne, Bowood Hall, Wiltshire. *Widener Collection*, 1942. Painted c. 1650. Canvas, 34½ x 41½" (87.5 x 105.5 cm.).

49

Of all the artists who have ever lived, Rembrandt was the greatest illustrator of the Bible. Where in art can one find the tenderness, the yearning faith, and at the same time the troubled puzzlement one sees in the face of Joseph of Arimethea, who grasps the body of Our Lord as He is lowered from the Cross? What painter has expressed pure, intense thought more clearly than Rembrandt does in the face and posture of St. Paul as he meditates on the letter he is about to write to his brothers in Christ? Rembrandt was drawn also to Roman history and legend, to which he brought his unique sense of theater. *Lucretia* (plate 52) would have been the envy of Sarah Bernhardt, or of any great actress, as she totters forward, dagger in hand, seeming to try to push away the dark fate that forces her to choose death over a life of dishonor.

50

51

52

REMBRANDT VAN RYN (Dutch 1606–1669)

49 *The Descent from the Cross.* Signed, and dated 165(1). Canvas, 56¼ x 43¾″ (143 x 111 cm.). Widener Collection

50 *The Circumcision.* Signed, and dated 1661. Canvas, 22¼ x 29½″ (56.5 x 75 cm.). Widener Collection

51 *The Apostle Paul.* Signed. Probably 1657. Canvas, 50¾ x 40⅛″ (129 x 102 cm.). Widener Collection.

52 *Lucretia.* Signed, and dated 1664. Canvas, 47¼ x 39¾″ (120 x 101 cm.). Andrew W. Mellon Collection

53 *Philemon and Baucis.* Signed, and dated 1658. Wood, 21½ x 27″ (54.5 x 68.5 cm.). Widener Collection

53

Jan Vermeer

(DUTCH, 1632–1675)

54 A LADY WRITING

Vermeer is now acclaimed one of the greatest artists who ever lived. A hundred years ago he was almost unknown, and he still remains among the most mysterious figures in the history of art. We have no letters, no diary, not a single line written by him. During his lifetime he is briefly mentioned in print only three times: first, in a poem saying he was a phoenix who rose from the ashes of Carel Fabritius, a fellow painter blown to bits by an explosion in Delft; a second time, in which only his name occurs; and a third mention in the diary of a French collector to whom he refused to show his paintings.

We do know, however, that he lived all his life in Delft, that he was a picture dealer, and that on one occasion he was called in as an expert to appraise some Italian paintings, which he said were rubbish. In 1652 he became a master and thus acquired the right to sell his own work. But amazingly he seems to have sold almost nothing. Paintings generally accepted as by him number fewer than forty, and of these it is thought that he still owned twenty-nine at the time of his death.

Vermeer must have painted slowly and painstakingly, completing only two or three pictures a year. His wife or one of his eleven children were his usual models. When he died he was deeply in debt, especially for food, which he must have needed for his hungry offspring.

Why, plagued with debt, was he so reluctant to part with his own work? There were certainly buyers for his pictures, for his style was not so original that collectors could not appreciate it. He painted like many of his contemporaries, only much better. Yet when a potential purchaser, Balthazar de Monconys, came all the way to Delft in 1663 to see him, he refused to show him anything. De Monconys relates how, after this rebuff, he was taken to a bakery where he saw a canvas with a single figure priced at three hundred florins, the same amount Dou, one of the most popular of Dutch painters, would customarily receive. There is reason to think that even this picture Vermeer had not sold but that the baker was holding it as collateral for debts.

Collections: Dr. Luchtmans, Rotterdam; J. Kamermans, Rotterdam; Count F. de Robiano, Brussels; J. Pierpont Morgan; Sir Harry Oakes. *Gift of Harry Waldron Havemeyer and Horace Havemeyer, Jr., in memory of their father, Horace Havemeyer, 1962. Signed. Painted c. 1665. Canvas, 17¾ x 15¾" (45 x 39.9 cm.).*

Jan Vermeer

(DUTCH, 1632–1675)

55 A WOMAN WEIGHING GOLD

Jan Vermeer of Delft was a master of stillness, of those moments of life when all action has ceased, held by an ephemeral adjustment of forces. This canvas conveys a sense of dynamic quiescence; it is in fact an allegory of balances. The unmoving figure weighing gold balances in her scales her earthly treasure, while Christ, in the Last Judgment in the background, in His divine knowledge weighs human guilt. The woman is absorbed, wrapped in the serene and mysterious thought of approaching maternity; and her pregnant body half concealing the painting hung behind her suggests a further equation, as though, as in Santayana's phrase, "The truth of life could be seen only in the shadow of death; living and dying were simultaneous and inseparable."

Such symbolic profundity is rare among Dutch painters of the seventeenth century and only intermittent in Vermeer's own work. The quality for which his paintings are always distinguished is form rather than content. For Vermeer among all Dutch artists is unrivaled in his mastery of optical reality. In his paintings just so much detail is included as can be seen from a normal distance, not by focusing the eye successively on different objects, or in an instant of time, but with a steady gaze. Similarly in his treatment of tone relations, there is a perfect consistency with what we actually see. No other painter has been able to maintain such subtle distinctions of color in different planes of light, or to extend this organization of tone into such depths of shadow.

Symmetry and balance in design, consistent selection of detail, proportional organization of tone relations, these are difficult to achieve, and Vermeer must have labored long and hard over each painting. Recently a Dutchman, van Meegeren, painted a series of religious pictures in the manner of Vermeer; but of these forgeries only one, *Supper at Emmaus*, is worthy of exhibition. The rest are so poor in quality that nothing but the chaos of the years of World War II could explain their temporary success. For Vermeer's mastery of optical truth cannot be imitated by the forger and is lost to some extent in the most faithful color reproduction.

Collections: Possibly in the collection of Jac. Abrahamsz. Dissius, Amsterdam; Nieuhof, Amsterdam; van der Bogaerd, Amsterdam; King of Bavaria, Munich; Duke of Caraman, Vienna and Paris; Casimir Périer; Comtesse de Ségur (née Périer) Paris. *Widener Collection*, 1942. Painted c. 1664. Canvas, 16¾ x 15" (42.5 x 38 cm.).

Claude Lorrain

(FRENCH, 1600-1682)

56 THE JUDGMENT OF PARIS

Unknown masterpieces still come to light. One day in 1966 a lady brought to Sotheby's, the London auction house, a dirty painting which she believed to be by the eighteenth-century English landscapist Richard Wilson. It was destined for a small sale, an unillustrated item in the catalogue, when one of the Sotheby partners noticed barely visible sheep in the foreground and realized that they looked like the sheep Claude often drew. The auctioneers, uncertain whether they were selling a copy, called in Marcel Röthlisberger, the greatest living authority on Claude Lorrain. With remarkable perspicacity he recognized under yellowed varnish and accumulated grime the touch of the master. When the landscape was sold, instead of a few thousand dollars it brought $480,000. The lady was indeed fortunate, and so was the dealer who bought the painting, for though its condition was scarcely discernible, when cleaned it proved to be excellently preserved.

It is, as Röthlisberger has said, "one of the most beautiful examples of classical landscape." Reproduced in Claude's *Liber Veritatis*, the book of drawings he made to authenticate his oeuvre, it contains figures larger than those of any other painting by him of like dimensions. They are considered entirely autograph, which cannot be said of the figures in many of his canvases, for in the words of Baldinucci, a contemporary, "he took no displeasure in having the figures in his landscapes or sea pieces added by another hand."

But it is not the figures, fine as these are, which entrance the viewer of this glorious landscape. It is the vista enframed on the right by one of the most magnificent trees Claude ever painted and balanced on the left by a steep, shadowy embankment. Here, in the far distance and in the middle ground, Claude enchants us, entraps our spirit in his Arcadian world. From the sweep of space in his paintings, from the way the eye glides to distant mountains and headlands, clear in shape but impalpable in substance, comes a curious psychological release, which both Dostoevski and Nietzsche have noted—an emotion difficult to describe but one which makes Claude, for some of us, the most satisfactory of all landscape painters.

Collections: Probably Marquis de Fontenay, Rome; recorded at auction sales in Paris, 1748, and London, 1819 and 1820; Miss V. Price, London. *Ailsa Mellon Bruce Fund,* 1969. Painted 1645/46. Canvas, 44¼ x 58⅞" (112 x 149.5 cm.).

Nicolas Poussin

(FRENCH, 1594-1665)

57 THE ASSUMPTION OF THE VIRGIN

This early work by Poussin is dependent on the past and predicts the future. On the one hand, it is strongly influenced by several paintings done a century earlier: Titian's *Assumption of the Virgin* and his Pesaro Altarpiece, both in the Church of the Frari in Venice, and his *Venus Worship*, now in the Prado but at that time in the Villa Aldobrandini in Frascati. On the other hand, it anticipates the freedom of brushwork and general exuberance which characterize the French Rococo. There are passages, especially in the painting of the chubby, rosy children, which might have been done by Fragonard.

It is difficult to imagine a more joyous Assumption than this. Three cherubs fill Our Lady's grave with flowers to take the place of her risen body. Accompanied aloft by swarms of other children who need no wings for their levitation, she looks upward in ecstasy while two of her entourage pull back the clouds as though they were draperies concealing Heaven. Poussin has achieved a miracle of movement, of twisting, turning *putti* that lead the eye toward a divine vision kept just out of sight. All this turbulence is controlled in turn by the verticals of two stately columns enframing the central scene and by the horizontals of the geometric sarcophagus in the foreground.

Such superb compositions are not easily arrived at. Poussin planned them carefully, often attaining his final design by placing on a miniature stage small figures which he moved around until he achieved the perfect balance of thrust and counterthrust. His intellectual approach to painting has made his work an inspiration to some of the best painters of our time. Picasso was greatly influenced by him, and the Cubists adopted many of his ideas on art, especially his emphasis on harmony, clarity, and, above all, reason.

But there is another side of Poussin as well. He could convey the sensuality of Titian and the great Venetians, a tradition continued in the eighteenth century in the work of Watteau, Fragonard, Boucher, and others, and in the nineteenth century in many artists from Delacroix to Renoir. It is an oversimplification to see the French School as a constant battle between the advocates of Rubens and the supporters of Raphael. Many of the greatest French artists, like Poussin, combined the richness of color and the fluency of brushwork of the one and the probity of draftsmanship and firmness of design of the other.

Collections: The Marquis of Exeter, Burghley House, at least as early as 1794, where it is said to have come from the Palazzo Soderini, Rome. *Ailsa Mellon Bruce Fund*, 1963. Painted c. 1626. Canvas, 52⅞ x 38⅝" (134.4 x 97.8 cm.).

Jean-Baptiste-Siméon Chardin

(FRENCH, 1699-1779)

58 THE ATTENTIVE NURSE

Chardin was the favorite painter of Diderot, whereas Boucher was the favorite, as we shall see, of Mme de Pompadour. The editor of the Encyclopedia had different taste from that popular at Versailles. He wished to see on canvas the virtues of domesticity rather than the enticements of femininity. In the long run, however, feminine charm is more tedious than domestic virtue, especially when this virtue is interpreted by Chardin's brush, which gilds with poetic light the everyday life of the middle class in eighteenth-century France.

For it was Chardin's talent to find plastic poetry in a bowl of fruit, a blue-and-white pitcher, or a nurse preparing a meal for her convalescent patient. In the picture reproduced here the painter conveys, with his exquisite sensibility, emotions of love and tenderness, sincere feelings springing from the charity in his heart but difficult to express without banality and triteness. Nothing could be further from the sometimes delicious and always glittering artificiality preferred at Versailles. Chardin was a product of Paris—the city of merchants and bankers, of traders and shopkeepers, of encyclopedists and bluestockings. His art is an affirmation of their independently developed taste, which at its best has a great appeal. But it was also a taste in which was latent that germ of sentimentality which a hundred years later became a plague that almost destroyed French painting.

Chardin's canvases also had considerable charm for the aristocracy. *The Attentive Nurse* was purchased from the artist by the Prince of Liechtenstein when he was Austrian Ambassador to France. It was one of the few works by Chardin that were not engraved before being sold, and it has been assumed that the Prince was so enamored of the picture, when it was displayed in the Salon of 1747, that he took it immediately to Vienna. Apart from a sketch which was probably the basis for Jules de Goncourt's etching, there are no other versions, which is unusual in Chardin's genre compositions of this type.

Collections: The Princes of Liechtenstein. *Samuel H. Kress Collection*, 1952. Signed. Painted probably 1738, the date which appears on its pendant, *The Governess*, in the National Gallery of Canada, Ottawa. Canvas, 18⅛ x 14½" (46.2 x 37 cm.).

François Boucher

(FRENCH, 1703-1770)

59   VENUS CONSOLING LOVE

Melancholy was a rare quality in the eighteenth century, especially in France. The overtones of sadness which lend such poetry to Watteau's work never appear in the paintings of Boucher. *Venus Consoling Love* once belonged to Mme de Pompadour. It is signed and dated 1751, the year Louis XV's mistress moved into a new apartment in the north wing of Versailles, where she was to live the rest of her life. It may have adorned these rooms or else have been painted for her château at Bellevue, where Boucher was working about 1750. He was Mme de Pompadour's favorite artist. She gave him commissions for innumerable decorations and easel pictures; ordered from him an illuminated prayer book, surprising as such a commission must seem; petted and cajoled him; and wrote her counselor of state that he must be kept in a good humor. For as she said, "I'm sure you would hate to find a crippled or cock-eyed nymph in your pretty room."

Mme de Pompadour has been said to have posed for the Venus in the painting reproduced here. But this entrancing maiden is much more the product of the painter's imagination. Boucher was never tied down to a model. He had learned a language of design, and this he used with the utmost freedom. Notice with what grace the movements of Venus, Cupid, and the surrounding *putti* are suggested. Or notice the lovely passages of painting in the feathers of the dove, the flowers, and the foliage. Eighteenth-century painters delighted in the display of beautiful handling, of fine brushwork, much as a violinist might take pleasure in a virtuoso performance. In this technical dexterity lies the principal charm of Rococo art.

Collections: Probably Mme de Pompadour and her brother, the Marquis de Ménars; H. Cousin, Paris; Baron Alfred de Rothschild, Buckinghamshire; Marchioness of Curzon, Kedleston, Derbyshire. *Gift of Chester Dale*, 1943. Signed, and dated 1751. Canvas, 42⅛ x 33⅜" (107 x 85 cm.).

Jean-Honoré Fragonard

(FRENCH, 1732-1806)

60   A YOUNG GIRL READING

Painted about 1776 at the peak of the artist's career, this charming study is considered by many critics to be among Fragonard's most appealing and masterly paintings. It is one of a series representing young girls in moments of solitude and relaxation, either reading a billet-doux, turning the pages of a book, or seated at a dressing table and lost in the world of their private thoughts. The identity of the sitters, as in this case, is unknown. Apparently Fragonard painted this series on speculation, hoping to interest Parisian patrons who were decorating their private apartments with intimate scenes typical of the last phase of Rococo taste.

Few paintings reveal more brilliantly that wonderful dexterity of brushwork for which Fragonard was famous. Look first at the curving fingers of the girl's hand holding the book. These fingers establish a rhythm which runs through the whole painting. The same movement, to be seen in various brushstrokes, is especially noticeable in the delicate and complicated touches which render the bows, the ribbons, and the ruffles of the young girl's costume. As in Boucher's *Venus Consoling Love* (plate 59), the quality of this brushwork has a spontaneity suggestive of a Mozartian cadenza. This virtuoso performance reaches a climax in the broad strokes of burnt umber which model the cushion and suggest its softly yielding volume. All these warm tones, placed so rapidly on the canvas, seem aglow with sunshine.

Collections: Leroy de Senneville, Paris; Duquesnoy, Paris; Marquis de Cypierre, Paris; Comte de Kergorlay, Paris; Ernest Cronier, Paris; Dr. Tuffier, Paris; Mr. and Mrs. Alfred W. Erickson, New York. *Gift of Mrs. Mellon Bruce in memory of her father, Andrew W. Mellon,* 1961. Painted c. 1776. Canvas, 32 x 25½" (81.1 x 64.8 cm.).

Francisco de Goya

(SPANISH, 1746–1828)

61 THE MARQUESA DE PONTEJOS

Until Picasso, Goya was the last of Spain's great painters. He was influenced, as were the American Colonial artists, by British painting. True, he knew the works of Gainsborough and Reynolds only in mezzotint engravings, but from prints after their portraits he learned to convey an impression of elegance and luxury. However, as a society portraitist in the English sense, his character was flawed. He could not take his sitters seriously. The Marquesa is just a little ridiculous. She is a fashion plate, as much the product of artificial selection as her pug dog. Her tulle skirt was more amusing to Goya than her insipid face. It offered him an opportunity to paint her portrait in a mockingly light palette with piquant alternations of sweet and acid colors.

In this work of Goya's early years there appears for the first time a note that is sardonic, even cynical. This was to swell to the terrifying chord, the clash of horror, the rumble of social systems in collapse that is heard with such fearful force in the great masterpieces of Goya's later years. This combination of a much deeper seriousness and a bitter disbelief in all established things provided a basis for those revolutions in painting which, under his influence, took place in France in the next century.

Collections: Marquesa de Martorell y de Pontejos, Madrid; Marqués de Miraflores y de Pontejos, Madrid. *Andrew W. Mellon Collection*, 1937. Painted possibly 1786. Canvas, 83 x 49¾" (211 x 126 cm.).

62

63

Goya's cynicism was nurtured at the Spanish court. Ruled over by an otiose king and a scheming queen, its corruption was appalling. Goya has depicted these two rulers as ugly manikins: he irresolute, she dissolute. In their miserable way they destroyed their niece, Doña María Teresa, later known as the Chinchón, whom Goya had painted as a beautiful child of almost three (plate 63). They forced her to marry Manuel Godoy. Godoy, the king's closest friend and trusted adviser, also happened to be the queen's lover and was by reputation the most depraved libertine at court. After experiencing her husband's infidelities and cruelty, the Chinchón sat for Goya again. This second likeness, which is owned by the Prado in Madrid, is the most melancholy portrait in existence.

64

66

65

Francisco de Goya (Spanish, 1746–1828)

62   *Carlos IV of Spain as Huntsman*. Probably 1799 or shortly after. Canvas, 18¼ x 11¾″ (46 x 30 cm.). Andrew W. Mellon Collection

63   *Condesa de Chinchón*. 1783. Canvas, 53 x 46¼″ (134.7 x 117.5 cm.). Ailsa Mellon Bruce Collection

64   *María Luisa, Queen of Spain*. Probably 1799 or shortly after. Canvas, 18¼ x 11¾″ (46 x 30 cm.). Andrew W. Mellon Collection

65   *Victor Guye*. 1810. Canvas, 42 x 33½″ (106.7 x 85.1 cm.). Gift of William Nelson Cromwell

66   *Don Antonio Noriega*. Signed, and dated 1801. Canvas, 40⅜ x 31⅞″ (102.6 x 80.9 cm.). Samuel H. Kress Collection

Thomas Gainsborough

(BRITISH, 1727-1788)

67 MRS. RICHARD BRINSLEY SHERIDAN

To understand this portrait, one must take into account its background in Whig society of the late eighteenth century—a society materialistic, rich, self-confident, yet with a love of learning and freedom and a special sensibility that sometimes verged on sentimentality. Mrs. Sheridan, the beautiful singer who married the wit, playwright, brilliant member of Parliament, and drunken favorite of Devonshire House, is a characteristic figure in that society. And this picture, at once charmingly pastoral (although nature is somewhat arranged, as the great Whig nobles liked it to be) and dashingly, artificially worldly, is a consummate expression of high Whig taste.

Gainsborough is known to have painted on occasion with brushes mounted on handles almost six feet long, in order to be the same distance from his model and his canvas. The consequent sketchiness of effect makes the certainty of each brushstroke still more remarkable. This feature of his style impressed Sir Joshua Reynolds, who wrote, "This chaos, this uncouth and shapeless appearance, by a kind of magic, at a certain distance assumes form, and all the parts seem to drop into their proper places; so that we can hardly refuse acknowledging the full effect of diligence, under the appearance of chance and hasty negligence."

Collections: Richard Brinsley Sheridan, Bath, England; Baron Nathaniel de Rothschild, Tring, Hertfordshire, and heirs, until sold by Lord Rothschild, London. *Andrew W. Mellon Collection*, 1937. Painted probably 1785/86. Canvas, 86½ x 60½" (220 x 154 cm.).

Sir Joshua Reynolds

(BRITISH, 1723-1792)

68 LADY CAROLINE HOWARD

In the portrait of Lady Caroline Howard, Reynolds has stressed a certain aspect of childhood, its innocence, its unstudied gracefulness. It does not matter that the portrait may not be a precise likeness of Lady Caroline, nor even that he used a similar pose and setting in other paintings of children, notably in *The Age of Innocence* in the National Gallery, London. For "the great aim of the art," as he said addressing the Royal Academy, "is to strike the imagination." In the portrait of Lady Caroline the mind is captured and converted to the romantic concept of childhood, "trailing clouds of glory," thirty years before Wordsworth's poem. Needless to say Reynolds himself was a bachelor!

Reynolds, in spite of the classical creed expounded in his *Discourses*, proves himself in many ways a precursor of the Romantics. This is manifest not only in his tendency to sentimentality but also in his faltering technique, in that uncertainty of craftsmanship which was the plague of Romantic painting. Thus many of his canvases, because of his constant technical experiments and his constant use of bitumen, have cracked and faded. *Lady Caroline Howard*, however, has lasted with its original brilliance and freshness; and for that reason it gives an idea of the luminosity of tone which must have characterized Reynolds' portraits when they left his studio, an impression hard to gain from many of his pictures in their present condition.

Collection: Earl of Carlisle, Castle Howard, England. *Andrew W. Melion Collection*, 1937. Painted c. 1778. Canvas, 56¼ × 44½" (143 × 113 cm.).

95

Sir Henry Raeburn

(BRITISH, 1756-1823)

69 MISS ELEANOR URQUHART

Flaubert's admonition to artists, "Be regular and ordinary in your life, like a bourgeois, so that you can be violent and original in your work," might serve as a description of Sir Henry Raeburn. Art was a business to this most distinguished of Scottish painters, and from nine to five-thirty it kept him regularly in his studio, where he painted a succession of three to four sitters a day. When he left his easel, it was to speculate in real estate or to play golf. But conventional as was his life, there was nothing conventional about his portraiture.

As a young man Raeburn decided to record only what he saw in front of him and never to trust his memory even when painting a subordinate part of the picture. This practice, common today, was contrary to the regular procedure of eighteenth-century portraitists. They used instead a preestablished tone for flesh, a traditional arrangement of highlights and shadows, and other fixed conventions. Raeburn, relying on actual observation and not on a memorized formula, developed a style which foreshadows contemporary painting.

For while he anticipates the goal of modern portraitists, seizing in his best works on the salient features of the sitter and rendering them in the moment of conception, his technical performance at times goes beyond the attainments of any contemporary artist. It is amazing that in portraying Miss Urquhart, for example, he did not have to change a single brushstroke. Success in direct painting of this type depends on the swiftness and certainty of the artist's hand. The moment he falters, renders a false shadow, fails to find the correct contour, misses the right color, the passage must be repainted and the freshness is gone.

Raeburn himself failed more often than he succeeded, and his work frequently suffers from the same faults that plague modern portraitists: either the pigment is thick from reworking, or the shadows too black, or the colors dull. *Miss Urquhart* is an exception; and it is easy to imagine that on this occasion, fascinated by the beauty of his sitter, the artist forgot all hesitations and afterthoughts and put down *à premier coup* the image of an aristocratic and charming woman, creating spontaneously one of his supreme masterpieces.

Collection: Captain Michael Pollard-Urquhart, Craigston, Scotland. *Andrew W. Mellon Collection,* 1937. Painted c. 1793. Canvas, 29⅜ x 24¼" (75 x 62 cm.).

Gilbert Stuart

(AMERICAN, 1755–1828)

70   THE SKATER

In two hundred years America has produced several great painters, and among these at least one innovator of genius, Gilbert Stuart. Stuart, who arrived in London in 1775, a penniless young student, was trained by his compatriot Benjamin West. In West's studio he was taught accepted methods of eighteenth-century portraiture: a general tint for flesh, certain fixed places for highlights and deep shadows, and, often to improve the appearance of the sitter, touches of carmine in the nostrils and the corners of the eyes.

The Skater, a portrait of William Grant of Congalton, was Gilbert Stuart's first of major importance. It was painted in London while he was still working in West's studio. At the time it was said that he had learned to make "a tolerable likeness of the face, but as to the figure he could not get below the fifth button." Possibly it was to overcome such criticism that he determined his portrait of William Grant should be full-length. The sittings were arranged, and one wintry day Grant remarked that the weather seemed more suitable for skating than for painting. Stuart agreed, and both went to skate in Hyde Park. The ice cracked, however, and they were forced to return. It was then that Stuart had an inspiration. He decided to portray his sitter on skates.

When *The Skater* was sent to the Royal Academy in 1782, according to Stuart's account it caused a sensation. Grant went there dressed in his skating costume, and Stuart described how the crowd followed him so closely he was compelled to make his retreat, for everyone was exclaiming, "That is he! That is the gentleman!" Although Stuart was apt to exaggerate, it is true the portrait was much admired.

Nearly a century later the unsigned *Skater* was again exhibited at the Royal Academy. Controversy over its authorship raged. The *Daily Telegraph* attributed it to Romney, but the *Times* said it was too good for that artist and suggested Hoppner or Raeburn. The *Art Journal* reported, "A more graceful and manly figure was surely never painted by an English artist, and if Gainsborough were that artist, this is unquestionably his masterpiece." This was the most logical assumption, as the sketchy landscape in the background, showing Westminster Abbey in the distance, is rendered very much in the manner of Gainsborough.

Again, for half a century, *The Skater* vanished from public attention. Fortunately, however, it was located and purchased by the National Gallery of Art. It remains uniquely important in Stuart's career, for as he observed to Josiah Quincy it is rare for an artist to be "suddenly lifted into fame by a single picture."

Collections: Inherited by William Grant's granddaughter, through whose marriage it came into the Pelham-Clinton family, Moor Park, Stroud, Gloucestershire, and London. *Andrew W. Mellon Collection*, 1950. Painted 1782. Canvas, 96⅝ x 58⅛" (245.3 x 147.6 cm.).

Gilbert Stuart

(AMERICAN, 1755-1828)

71 MRS. RICHARD YATES

To quote a contemporary, Dunlap, soon after painting *The Skater* Stuart had "his full share of the best business in London, and prices equal to any, except Sir Joshua Reynolds and Gainsborough." But his earnings could not keep pace with his expenditures. Deeply in debt, he returned to America and spent the rest of his life painting the heroes of the new Republic and the increasingly wealthy merchants and their families.

He once said, "I want to find out what nature is for myself, and see her with my own eyes." Such freshness of vision was easier to achieve in the Colonies than in the mother country, for in America no formula for painting had yet been established. Patrons like Mrs. Yates, the wife of a New York merchant, wanted to see themselves as they really were, and they were perfectly willing that an artist should make technical experiments if these led to a more accurate portrayal. Thus, after his return to America in 1793, Stuart's power of observation increased, and he noted, among other facts of vision, that "good flesh coloring partook of all colors, not mixed, so as to be combined in one tint, but shining through each other, like the blood through the natural skin." Had there been the artists and the tradition of painting in America that there were in France, these innovations of Stuart's might have caused Impressionism to appear in the New World generations before it revolutionized art in Europe.

Collections: Carlisle Pollock II, grandson of the sitter, New Orleans; and by descent to Mrs. Louise Chiapella Formento; Dr. Isaac M. Cline, New Orleans; Thomas B. Clarke, New York. *Andrew W. Mellon Collection*, 1940. Painted 1793/94. Canvas, 30¼ x 25" (77 x 63 cm.).

John Singleton Copley

(AMERICAN, 1738-1815)

72   THE COPLEY FAMILY

The career of John Singleton Copley, the greatest American artist of the eighteenth century, was the reverse of that of Stuart. Copley got his start in Boston and did not settle in London, where he spent the rest of his life, until 1775.

His wife's father, Richard Clarke, was a consignee of the famous shipment of tea which was sent to America contrary to the wishes of the Colonists, only to be thrown into the harbor in the Boston Tea Party. Consequently Clarke, a loyal Tory merchant, left the Colonies in high dudgeon and low repute, taking with him Copley's family. Copley, who had been studying in Italy for a year, soon joined his family in London. Shortly after his arrival he painted the group portrait reproduced here.

Mrs. Copley and her father sit in the foreground, surrounded by the little Copleys, while the artist looks out pensively from behind and clutches all that remains of his New England prosperity—a few sheets of drawings. Copley had reached a crossroads in his life. He was settled in England, faced with the necessity of making his way in an alien country where standards were very different from those he had left behind in Boston. He decided to change his whole approach to portraiture. *The Copley Family* shows, side by side, his old and his new styles. The painting of his father-in-law, especially his face and hands, and the charmingly rendered doll in the corner of the picture are the last echoes of that visual truth which characterized his early work. The painting of his wife, of the children, the composition of the picture, all are reminiscent of Reynolds, of West, of the "grand manner" of portraiture, which Copley forced himself to adopt. For a period he was successful and was elected a member of the Royal Academy, but he fell out of fashion. And though he painted more industriously than ever, he was unable to gain back his reputation. The end of his life was sad, for he was constantly menaced by debts and seems to have felt that he had betrayed his original gifts.

Collections: Copley family, London and Boston. *Andrew W. Mellon Fund*, 1961. Painted 1776/77. Canvas, 72½ x 90⅜" (184.4 x 229.7 cm.).

John Constable

(BRITISH, 1776-1837)

73 WIVENHOE PARK, ESSEX

One function of art is to suggest a world perfectly attuned to human desires. During the Renaissance this earthly paradise was usually located in Greece, in a pastoral country known as Arcadia. Today the English countryside of a century or more ago has something of the same nostalgic appeal for us that the Hellenic world had for the humanists of the Renaissance. However, Arcadian shepherds are imaginary figures, whereas we know from a host of novelists how real was the English squirearchy, how actual its serene and stable environment.

"Arcadian realism" may seem a contradictory term, but it describes the charm of many of Constable's canvases. His scenes are filled with poetry, visions of the tranquil delight of an ideal rural existence. Yet, at the same time, they have an extraordinary reality, conveying as they do flashes of insight into the momentary moods of nature with that sensibility which is at the heart of modern landscape painting.

In a letter written in 1816 by Constable to his future wife, we sense how much owners of estates like Wivenhoe Park must have esteemed their possessions. "My dearest Love," Constable wrote, "I have been here since Monday and am as happy as I can be away from you. . . . I am going on very well with my pictures. The park is the most forward. The great difficulty has been to get so much in as they [the Rebows] wanted . . . so that my view comprehended too many degrees. But today I got over the difficulty and I begin to like it myself."

The wish of the owner to see as much as possible of his estate explains the unusually wide angle of the artist's view. But Constable, by the actuality he gives *Wivenhoe Park*, triumphs over this difficult composition and makes us agree with General Rebow that it would not be possible to see too much of so entrancing a scene. So there is no necessity for the twilight with which earlier landscapists gave a romantic aspect to their Arcadian scenery. Instead, Constable has found in a typical English day of scattered clouds and brilliant sunshine a new inspiration. He reveals "the infinite variety of natural appearances," and delights in the loveliness of flickering, sparkling light as it falls on leaves and grass and water. Painting was changed by such a fresh observation of landscape, just as poetry was changed at about the same time by Wordsworth's descriptions of nature.

Collection: Wivenhoe Park, Essex. *Widener Collection*, 1942. Painted 1816. Canvas, 22⅛ x 39⅞" (56.1 x 101.2 cm.).

Joseph Mallord William Turner

(BRITISH, 1775–1851)

74 MORTLAKE TERRACE

In 1827 Turner exhibited at the Royal Academy the picture reproduced here, which was titled *Mortlake Terrace, the Seat of William Moffatt, Esq.; Summer's Evening.* The preceding year he had exhibited the same site seen from the opposite direction and bathed in the light of an early summer morning, a picture now in the Frick Collection in New York. These two canvases were executed at a moment of significant change in Turner's style: a period when light and the rendering of a visible atmosphere were becoming his preoccupation, to the exclusion of his earlier interest in topography. Though he was doubtless fulfilling a commission in depicting Moffatt's garden terrace from opposite points and under contrasting illumination, Turner's whole effort was concentrated on the atmospheric envelope of the scene, on rendering the sun-filled mist of a hot afternoon. As one of the most astute of French critics, Théophile Thoré (W. Bürger), wrote in 1865, "Everything seems to be luminous with its own light and to throw its own rays and sparks. Claude, the master of luminosity, has never done anything so prodigious!"

How little Turner worried at this time about the design of his paintings is illustrated by the story of the dog on the parapet. The anecdote is recorded by Frederick Goodall, whose father engraved some of Turner's pictures. On Varnishing Day at the Royal Academy when Turner was out for lunch, Edwin Landseer, the animal painter, came in and noticed *Mortlake Terrace.* He saw at once that it needed an accent in the center, and so he cut out of paper a little dog and stuck it on the parapet. "When Turner returned," Goodall says, "he went up to the picture quite unconcernedly, never said a word, adjusted the little dog perfectly, and then varnished the paper and began painting it. And there it is to the present day." There is no doubt that the composition of the painting was saved by this accidental but highly successful collaboration, one of the most unusual in the history of art.

Collections: Perhaps William Moffatt, owner of Mortlake Terrace; Joseph Hamatt; Rev. Edward J. Daniel; Thomas Creswick, R.A.; E. B. Fripp; Samuel Ashton; Thomas Ashton; Mrs. Elizabeth Gair Ashton. *Andrew W. Mellon Collection,* 1937. Painted c. 1826. Canvas, 36¼ x 48⅛" (92 x 122.2 cm.).

Jacques-Louis David

(FRENCH, 1748–1825)

75 NAPOLEON IN HIS STUDY

How much our concept of historic personages depends upon the artists who portrayed them! Compared to Napoleon, a man like Doge Gritti (see plate 24), for example, was insignificant. Yet no one who painted the Emperor was able to give him an appearance of authority, of human grandeur. Perhaps Napoleon lived too late. The available artists were incapable of creating an image commensurate with his achievement. David tried, but has managed merely to supply a mass of external trappings.

The Emperor's uniform combines details of the Grenadiers of his famous Imperial Guard with an infantry general's epaulettes, a uniform worn by him on Sundays and special occasions. His medals are the insignia of the Legion of Honor and the Iron Cross of Italy, two orders which he himself had created. Beneath the table is a copy of Plutarch's *Lives*. The manuscript of the *Code Napoléon* is on the desk. The pen and scattered papers, the candles burning to their sockets, and the clock pointing to a quarter-past four, all indicate that the Emperor has just finished a hard night's work. This unmitigated flattery caused the Emperor to say to the artist, "You have understood me, David. By night I work for the welfare of my subjects, and by day for their glory."

Just as the portrait of Gritti probably held a special significance for Charles I, so this portrait of Napoleon, a masterpiece of political propaganda, must have had its own meaning for another Briton, the Duke of Hamilton, who looked upon himself as descended from James I and thus the rightful heir to the throne of Scotland. A Catholic, a Scottish nationalist, and a close friend of Napoleon's sister, Pauline Bonaparte, he considered the Emperor a potential ally in the restoration of the Stuarts. In his gallery the portrait of the archenemy of his country, which he had commissioned David to paint, was predominant.

Although the painting is signed and dated 1812, David's grandson said it was painted in Paris in 1810. But the correct date is established by the chair designed by David himself and delivered in 1812, as well as by correspondence which shows that the portrait was being worked on in the winter of that year, shortly before Napoleon embarked on his fatal Russian invasion. There were supposed to be four replicas of the Hamilton portrait, but only one, belonging to Prince Napoleon, can be definitely identified.

Collections: Marquess of Douglas (Alexander, tenth Duke of Hamilton), Hamilton Palace, near Glasgow; Archibald Philip, fifth Earl of Rosebery; Albert Edward, sixth Earl of Rosebery, London. *Samuel H. Kress Collection*, 1961. Signed, and dated 1812. Canvas, 80¼ x 49¼" (203.9 x 125.1 cm.).

Jean-Auguste-Dominique Ingres

(FRENCH, 1780–1867)

76   MADAME MOITESSIER

Fashion in feminine beauty is as variable as fashion in clothes. Occasionally this mutability of taste affects the appreciation of a work of art. Many people today, for example, would consider Mme Moitessier, as she appears in her portrait by Ingres, an ugly woman, corpulent and bovine. Their dislike of her appearance might even blind them to the merits of the painting. Yet to Ingres, the outstanding master of the French academic school, she was the reincarnation of a goddess of the ancient world, an archetype of the beautiful woman.

Although the portraitist often extolled his sitter's appearance, he seems to have had only a secondary interest in her personality. He worked for months on her portrait, finishing the dress and accessories; then he added the arms and hands; and finally he attached the head to the bare shoulders. Painting backward, so to speak, he treated his picture less as portraiture than as still life, and concentrated his immense virtuosity on painting Mme Moitessier's clothes, jewels, fan, and beside her the chair with gloves and fur jacket. It is Ingres' marvelous conjunction of eye and hand in such passages, the way he renders the subtle ellipses of flesh in the fat arms, the depth of translucence in the rubies and sapphires, the sheen of the pearl necklace, the subtle distinction between the gilt of the chair and the gold of the bracelets, that shows his mastery of realistic detail. This verisimilitude has remained, on his example, the principal goal of academic painting.

Character is certainly lacking in Mme Moitessier's somnolent face, but her cold and symmetrical beauty offered Ingres a solution to a conflict at the heart of his style. He was both a classicist and a realist; consequently his selective instinct impelled him toward models who recalled the canons of classical proportion, as we know them from the sculpture of Greece or Rome, and he was really happy only when depicting people who approached this ideal. Once at the opera a pupil, seeing the master restless and obviously disturbed, asked whether he did not admire the tenor's voice. "Yes, yes," Ingres answered, "it's a beautiful voice and beautifully produced but . . . his eyes are rather wide apart!" In looking at Mme Moitessier, however, he found no such fault. Her regular features and ample figure were an inspiration and a challenge. Théophile Gautier, the French critic, wrote after watching her pose for this portrait: "Never did beauty more regal, more magnificent, more stately, and of a more Junoesque type, offer its proud lines to the tremulous pencil of an artist."

Collections: M. and Mme Sigisbert Moitessier; Comtesse de Flavigny (née Moitessier); Vicomtesse O. de Bondy (née Moitessier); Comte Olivier de Bondy, Château de la Barre (Indre). *Samuel H. Kress Collection,* 1946. Signed, and dated 1851. Canvas, 57¾ x 39½" (146.7 x 100.3 cm.).

Eugène Delacroix

(FRENCH, 1798–1863)

77 ARABS SKIRMISHING IN THE MOUNTAINS

In 1832 Delacroix was attached to a French military mission sent to the Sultan of Morocco. His journey lasted five months. He arrived in Tangier exhausted from the competitive struggle which had marked his life since the Revolution of 1830. He had lost his appetite for work and was much in need of the refreshment and inspiration of new scenes. These he found in North Africa. He wrote a friend, "The thought of my reputation, of that Salon which I was supposed to be missing, never occurs to me. I'm even sure that the considerable sum of curious information that I shall bring back from here will be of little use to me. Away from the land where I discovered them, such particulars will be like trees torn from their native soil; my mind will have forgotten its impressions, and I shall disdain to give a cold and imperfect rendering of the living and striking sublimity that lies all about one here."

He was wrong. His mind always retained its impressions of North Africa. His sketches in the Louvre, small and fragile as they are, remain among the great treasures of French art. Throughout his life he turned to them repeatedly. *Arabs Skirmishing in the Mountains*, for example, was painted thirty-one years after his visit to Morocco, a few months before his death. It was his last important easel picture and was shown in the Centennial Exhibition of 1863.

Delacroix's feelings about the Arabs were ambivalent. In one letter just after his arrival he wrote, "This place is made for painters. . . ." By contrast, a month later he wrote, "I have spent most of my time here in utter boredom, because it was impossible to draw anything from nature openly, even the meanest hovel; if you so much as go on to the terrace you run the risk of being stoned or shot at. The Moors are fantastically jealous, and it is on these terraces that their women usually take the air or visit one another." But time alchemized these days of boredom into golden memories. He recalled the strong colors, the blinding light, the violence, all of which appealed deeply to his nature. In recollection he saw these Arabs as romantic heroes, fierce and courageous warriors, as wild and unbroken as their beautiful horses.

In 1865 Delacroix's first biographer wrote that the battle scene in the picture reproduced here represented a fight between tax collectors and their reluctant victims. As far as one can judge, the Sultan's emissaries are losing. But how much more picturesque they are than their tamer yet never defeated colleagues today! It has often amused me to think that this violent resistance to tax collecting now hangs a few blocks from the United States Bureau of Internal Revenue.

Collections: Edouard André, Paris; A. Smit, Paris; C. D. Borden, New York; James J. Hill, St. Paul; Louis W. Hill, St. Paul; Jerome Hill, New York. *Chester Dale Fund*, 1966. Signed, and dated 1863. Canvas, 36⅜ x 29⅜" (92.5 x 74.6 cm.).

Jean-Baptiste-Camille Corot

(FRENCH, 1796-1875)

78 AGOSTINA

Time may prove Corot to have been the most important painter of the nineteenth century. Certainly the admiration he has aroused in other artists has been unceasing, and his influence even on contemporary artists like Picasso, immense. He was one of the few artists of recent times to excel not only in landscape but also in figure painting, of which *Agostina* is an outstanding example. Here he combines an alertness of vision with a profound knowledge of Renaissance style. This Italian peasant girl, who stands with unself-conscious detachment, evokes the heroic women of Piero della Francesca. But she is also of her own century, for she has been observed by the artist with an enamored and penetrating scrutiny which brings her much closer to actuality, to the living model, than her fifteenth-century forebears.

The plastic values which distinguish Corot's best landscapes are due in part to his constant study of human form. This is of importance in understanding his work. There is a profound difference in style between those landscape painters who are either incapable of drawing the human form, or draw it in a perfunctory way, and those whose art is based on a knowledge of the body. In one category we have artists like Perugino, Claude Lorrain, most of the Dutch landscape painters with the significant exception of Rembrandt, and, in the nineteenth century, Turner and Monet, among others. All these artists could draw the human figure after a fashion, but none of them was a figure painter of any consequence. In their landscapes we find that such effects as the sweep of distance and the play of light are stressed, but in the beautiful iridescent spaces they create, everything is insubstantial, intangible. The other category, those artists like Corot who have mastered the hollows and bosses of the human form, its plastic shape, seem able to translate this knowledge of mass and volume into hills and rocks and trees. Painters like Rubens, Poussin, Rembrandt, Cézanne, and, at his best, Corot are intent on rendering the plastic character of nature. They model trees and rocks with the same studious gravity they show toward the human body. They seem to be in search of the tendons and sinews of nature.

Collections: Breysse, Paris; Faure, Paris; Paton, Paris; Bernheim-Jeune, Paris. *Chester Dale Collection*, 1962. Signed. Painted probably 1866. Canvas, 52¼ x 38⅜" (132.8 x 97.6 cm.).

Honoré Daumier

(FRENCH, 1808–1879)

79   **ADVICE TO A YOUNG ARTIST**

Corot's figure style influenced the work of his close companion, Daumier. The two artists had much in common—both sought and found the true tradition of painting in the Italian masters. Balzac said of Daumier, "He is a man who has something of Michelangelo in his blood." But this great talent had to be lavished on caricatures for various periodicals. Poverty left Daumier little time for painting, and with failing eyesight he could not draw and sell his famous cartoons fast enough to pay his rent, even for the dilapidated cottage he occupied at Valmondois. But he was fortunate in one thing—in friendship. Corot secretly bought Daumier's house, and wrote him as follows: "My old comrade—I had a little house for which I had no use at Valmondois near the Isle-Adam. The idea came into my head of offering it to you, and as I think it is a good idea, I have placed it in your name at the notary's. It is not for you that I do this, it is merely to annoy your landlord." It was a simple gesture, and it gave Daumier a few serene and tranquil years. But it meant that Corot painted fewer Agostinas and more misty lakes, fewer masterpieces and more potboilers. In return for this sacrifice, a few paintings like this, which once belonged to Corot, were all that Daumier could give his old friend, but into their execution he poured all the brilliant genius that a lifetime of poverty could not destroy.

Collections: J.-B.-C. Corot, Paris; Adolphe A. Tavernier, Paris; Cronier, Paris; Goerg, Rheims. *Gift of Duncan Phillips*, 1941. Signed. Painted probably after 1860. Canvas, 16⅛ x 12⅞" (41 x 33 cm.).

Edouard Manet

(FRENCH, 1832-1883)

80   THE OLD MUSICIAN

The principal pleasure to be gained from Manet comes from the beauty of his brushwork. He mixed on his palette the exact tone he needed and with swift and certain dexterity delineated on the canvas each area of light and shadow. In *The Old Musician* this virtuosity of handling can be seen most clearly in the trenchant strokes that define the folds in the shirt and trousers of the boy with the straw hat, or in the more caressing feather touch on the shawl of the girl holding the baby.

Manet's method of direct painting caused him to suppress the transitional tones of modeling which particularly suggest volume. Like Velázquez, who was also a master of brushwork, he chose an illumination which would flatten form as much as possible. Thus the light falls directly on the figures from behind the artist's head, and the shadows are reduced to a minimum. Through this arbitrary elimination of shadow Manet was able to state local color more freely. He attained, especially in such early works as *The Old Musician*, the most subtle harmonies of yellowish white and faded blue, here contrasted with warm browns and blacks and soft grays. This color scheme was as far as possible from the high intensities and broken colors of the Impressionists, which he adopted at the end of his life.

For Manet, in spite of a strong instinct for the traditional, became a leader of the Impressionists' revolt. The public attacked his pictures, as they attacked the other Impressionists, but less because of his method of painting than because of a certain outré quality in his subject matter. In *The Old Musician*, for instance, what is the meaning of the brooding octogenarian on the extreme right, who is bisected so unconventionally by the frame? Perhaps he was put there simply to balance the composition, for Théodore Duret, who knew Manet well, said he painted this troupe of beggars merely because it pleased him to preserve a record of them and for no other reason. And yet one senses a significance which just escapes, a hidden meaning which is baffling. In Manet's pictures these recurrent and tantalizing affectations infuriated his contemporaries and were in part the reason he never attained the popular admiration which he so desperately desired.

Collections: Manet family, Paris; Prince de Wagram, Paris; P. R. Pearson, Paris; Kunsthistorisches Museum, Vienna. *Chester Dale Collection*, 1962. Signed, and dated 1862. Canvas, 73¾ x 98" (187.5 x 249.1 cm.).

Edouard Manet

(FRENCH, 1832–1883)

81   GARE SAINT-LAZARE

Why does this painting convey such a sense of gaiety? There is, of course, the marvelous observation of the little sleeping dog, one of the most enchanting puppies in art. There is also the pretty Victorine Meurend, whose beauty is more familiar to us from pictures of ten years earlier, *Olympia* and *Le Déjeuner sur l'herbe*. Dressed or undressed she is a joy, delighting us with the wonderfully candid gaze of a woman to whom shyness is unknown. But the real source of our pleasure, the heroine of the picture, is the little girl, the daughter of Manet's friend Alphonse Hirsch. From the way she holds the railing, from the angle of her head, from the beautiful line made by the curve of her neck, we know the intensity of her scrutiny. We share the excitement we felt in childhood at seeing trains and steam and smoke. Manet knew better than anyone else how to catch the fugitive charm of everyday life. He was a master of the informal composition. He had a keen sense of the immediacy this type of design can convey. The *Gare Saint-Lazare* is a family snapshot. But this moment of time, made timeless, is held with a beauty and intensity far beyond the possibilities of photography.

The painting was admitted, somewhat unexpectedly, to the Salon of 1874, where it aroused more protests than praise. It was the first large canvas Manet had executed mostly out-of-doors, perhaps acknowledging thereby his association with the younger Impressionists, Monet and Renoir especially, who had for some time been working in the open air. Thus it carried into the citadel of the official Salon the banner of their revolt.

Collections: Jean-Baptiste Faure, Paris; Havemeyer family, New York. *Gift of Horace Havemeyer in memory of his mother, Louisine W. Havemeyer,* 1956. Signed, and dated 1873. Canvas, 36¾ x 45⅛″ (93.3 x 114.5 cm.).

121

Auguste Renoir

(FRENCH, 1841–1919)

82   A GIRL WITH A WATERING CAN

A Girl with a Watering Can, painted in 1876, is one of the most popular pictures in the National Gallery. It is evocative of sunlight and childhood, springtime and the breath of flowers, images and sensations which are in themselves attractive. But these are not enough. To be great a painting must have more than charm of subject matter; it must have certain aesthetic values as well. In the case of *A Girl with a Watering Can*, these values consist largely in the relationship of figure and landscape, in the way the two are fused by ingenious repetition of colors and a consistent treatment of detail. The whole picture is made up of a web of brilliantly colored brushstrokes, which from a distance are seen to be a child, roses, grass, a garden path. The little girl seems to merge with her surroundings, to become one with the variegated tones of nature. This creates a mysterious sense of interrelations, as though one substance permeated humanity, vegetation, and earth.

The unity of figure and background Renoir extends to a psychological unity between himself and the child. The scene is depicted from the level of the little girl's own vision, so that her outlook on nature is suggested. Thus the garden becomes the world seen through her eyes, narrow and circumscribed. By accepting her scale of observation, Renoir evokes, in an almost unique way, memories of childhood. This mood, this "remembrance of things past," is intensified by the pleasure of the painter in his subject, by the spontaneity and gaiety of his treatment of the scene. Renoir, in canvases like this, seems almost a pagan Fra Angelico. "I arrange my subject as I want it," he once said, "and then I go ahead and paint it like a child." He loved bright colors, joyous and pretty human beings, and nature drenched in sunshine. He was a painter moved to lyrical ecstasy by the beauty of the everyday world. His great gift was to catch on canvas

A strain of the earth's sweet being in the beginning . . .
Innocent mind and Mayday in girl and boy.

Collections: Paul Bérard, Paris; A. Rosenberg, Paris; Prince de Wagram, Paris. *Chester Dale Collection*, 1962. Signed, and dated 1876. Canvas, 39½ x 28¾″ (100 x 73 cm.).

Edgar Degas

(FRENCH, 1834-1917)

83   MADAME RENÉ DE GAS

Some of the greatest paintings done by Degas, curiously enough, were painted in America, for he spent the winter of 1872–73 in New Orleans. His mother had been born there, and his uncle and brothers had established themselves in that city as cotton merchants. In a letter he describes his gratitude to one of his brothers, René, whose wife appears in the painting reproduced here. "I knew neither English nor the art of traveling in America; therefore I obeyed [René] blindly. What stupidities I should have committed without him! He is married and his wife, our cousin, is blind, poor thing, almost without hope. She has borne him two children, she is going to give him a third whose godfather I shall be, and as the widow of a young American killed in the War of Secession she already had a little girl of her own who is 9 years old."

With tactful subtlety Degas has suggested the blind, unfocused stare of his sister-in-law. The portrait seems unposed, the sitter unself-conscious. Thus Degas conveys that feeling of fortuitous objectivity which was his goal in portraiture. As he once said, he was interested in doing "portraits of people in familiar and typical attitudes, above all giving to their faces the same choice of expression as one gives to their bodies." Consequently, he sought to transcribe appearance accurately, to achieve photographic veracity, as though the camera had just clicked and the artist had transposed to the canvas his exact mental picture. But though the casual yet perfectly balanced design of this picture has the immediacy of a snapshot, the artist, because draftsmanship is more flexible than photography, has been able to eliminate all extraneous detail and to concentrate attention on the important features of his sitter. Unfortunately, contemporary portraiture has lost the secret of combining aesthetic perception with photographic likeness.

Collections: Degas' atelier until 1918; Henry D. Hughes, Philadelphia. *Chester Dale Collection*, 1962. Atelier stamp: Degas. Painted in the winter of 1872–73. Canvas, 28⅝ x 36¼" (72.7 x 92 cm.).

84

Edgar Degas (French, 1834–1917)

84 *Girl Drying Herself.* Signed, and dated 1885. Pastel, 31½ x 20⅛" (80.1 x 51.2 cm.). Gift of the W. Averell Harriman Foundation in memory of Marie N. Harriman

85 *Before the Ballet.* Signed. 1888. Canvas, 15¾ x 35" (40 x 89 cm.). Widener Collection

86 *Dancers at the Old Opera House.* Signed. c. 1877. Pastel, 8⅝ x 6¾" (21.8 x 17.1 cm.). Ailsa Mellon Bruce Collection

87 *Ballet Dancers.* Signed. c. 1877. Pastel and gouache, 11¾ x 10⅝" (29.7 x 26.9 cm.). Ailsa Mellon Bruce Collection

88 *Ballet Scene.* c. 1907. Pastel on cardboard, 30¼ x 43¾" (76.8 x 111.2 cm.). Chester Dale Collection

89 *Dancers Backstage.* Signed. c. 1890. Canvas, 9½ x 7⅜" (24.2 x 18.8 cm.). Ailsa Mellon Bruce Collection

Degas was a master at discovering beauty in the world around him. He particularly loved the opera and the ballet, but he loved them for professional reasons—for the fleeting gesture, the significance given to a passing moment. In the performance or the rehearsals of the ballerinas he found a kaleidoscope of shifting forms, which stimulated his sense of design. In the reproductions in this volume, especially in *Ballet Scene* (plate 88), a pastel painted in his last years, he reveals the plasticity of these young bodies and the motion of their complicated postures as no other artist has ever done.

85

86

87

89

88

90

91

92

Working out-of-doors, Monet found that colors were constantly changing. To analyze these changes, he decided to paint a single subject at different times of day under different illumination. In over thirty canvases he showed how the color of Rouen Cathedral varies depending on the light that falls on it. Two of these Rouen paintings are reproduced here. A second observation, illustrated in all these reproductions, is that shadow is not colorless, is not brown or black, but is simply a less bright hue.

Claude Monet (French, 1840–1926)

90 *Rouen Cathedral, West Façade.* Signed, and dated 1894. Canvas, 39½ x 26″ (100.4 x 66 cm.). Chester Dale Collection

91 *Rouen Cathedral, West Façade, Sunlight.* Signed, and dated 1894. Canvas, 39½ x 26″ (100.2 x 66 cm.). Chester Dale Collection

92 *Bridge at Argenteuil on a Gray Day.* Signed. c. 1876. Canvas, 24 x 31⅝″ (61 x 80.3 cm.). Ailsa Mellon Bruce Collection

93 *Argenteuil.* Signed. c. 1872. Canvas, 19⅞ x 25⅝″ (50.4 x 65.2 cm.). Ailsa Mellon Bruce Collection

94 *Ships at Anchor on the Seine.* Signed. 1872/73. Canvas, 14⅞ x 18⅛″ (37.8 x 46.6 cm.). Ailsa Mellon Bruce Collection

95 *The Artist's Garden at Vétheuil.* Signed, and dated 1880. Canvas, 59⅝ x 47⅝″ (151.4 x 121 cm.). Ailsa Mellon Bruce Collection

93

95

Paul Cézanne

(FRENCH, 1839–1906)

96   THE ARTIST'S FATHER

It is hard to imagine a more ambivalent relationship than that of Paul Cézanne and his father. Emile Zola, Paul's closest friend, describes the elder Cézanne as "mocking, republican, bourgeois, cold, meticulous, stingy. . . . He is, moreover, garrulous and, sustained by his wealth, doesn't care a rap for anyone or anything." This was probably also the younger Cézanne's judgment when in 1866 he was painting the portrait reproduced here; and yet twenty years later, according to friends, he venerated his parent, who had left him what he considered to be a large income.

Louis-Auguste Cézanne started his life as a manufacturer of hats, and by 1848 he had made enough money to buy the local bank, which was in financial difficulties because of the Revolution. He restored its prosperity and hoped his son, too, would become a banker. But when banking made Paul so obviously unhappy, and all he could think of was painting, his father gave him an allowance, small but sufficient to enable him to follow his unprofitable profession. He even agreed to act as a model for his son, whose work he never understood.

With time, relations between father and son, always variable, worsened, and the nadir was reached in 1872 when Paul had a son by Hortense Fiquet. His father was willing to support Paul as a bachelor but unwilling to have a family kept at his expense, especially one his son would not acknowledge. Yet eventually he accepted even this, and in 1886 when Paul at last married Hortense he signed the register. He could scarcely have objected to the long period of illegitimacy of his grandson, since he himself had not married until his own son, Paul, was five years old.

Paul Cézanne painted his father at least three times and drew him often. Of these likenesses the National Gallery portrait is the most overwhelming. The massive body of the sitter, slightly turned in his armchair, suggests such weight and solidity, gives such an effect of three-dimensional existence, that it is difficult to find a comparable portrait by any other artist. These formal qualities are linked to an indefinable tenderness, "as though," to quote John Rewald, "while contemplating him, often without the model's knowledge, the painter had felt the deep-rooted links that nature or fate had established between him and this old man."

Father and son always shared a certain toughness—a revulsion for all sentimentality. When the banker was trying to persuade his son to give up painting, he used to say, "Think of the future; one dies with genius, but one eats with money." After his father's death, Paul, perhaps with subconscious irony, altered this aphorism into his only eulogy for his parent: "My father was a man of genius; he left me an income of twenty-five thousand francs."

Collections: Auguste Pellerin, Paris; Mme René Lecomte, Paris. *Collection of Mr. and Mrs. Paul Mellon*, 1970. Painted 1866. Canvas, 78⅛ x 47" (198.5 x 119.3 cm.).

131

Paul Cézanne

(FRENCH, 1839–1906)

97 HOUSE OF PÈRE LACROIX

Paul Cézanne's life was consecrated to painting. In his lonely retreat at Aix he once wrote to Emile Bernard, "I have sworn to die painting"; and he carried out his vow, for he was found after a torrential downpour of rain, unconscious beside his easel. A passerby carried him home in a laundry cart; yet the next morning he struggled back to his studio, was again stricken, and died a few days later.

What was the vision he followed with such passion and such relentlessness? As nearly as words can describe such matters, his quest was twofold: to discover a means of transcribing the weft of color that in nature covers and yet indicates mass, and to find a way of conveying an impression of space without destroying these color relations. In the present landscape, for example, which he painted at Auvers, near Paris, in 1873, he wished to show the trees and the walls of the cottages not only as the colored patterns of light and shade which would have satisfied an Impressionist painter but also to communicate his perception of their volumes, the dense mass of the foliage and the solidity of the buildings. Similarly, he wished to transcend Impressionism in the rendering of space. Instead of allowing the colors to fade into a misty background, the conventional method of suggesting recession, he wanted to maintain chromatic intensity even in the distance. Thus local color in the *House of Père Lacroix* retains its strength in every plane; and space is created not by diminution of tonal contrast but by the position and scale of the trees, the cottages, and the hill which make up the scene. The magic of Cézanne's style consists in his power to suggest, through selection of color and organization of form, solid volumes in a sequence of planes, aspects of vision which we experience more intensely in his paintings than we do when we look directly at nature.

Collections: Alphonse Kann, St.-Germain-en-Laye, France; Auguste Pellerin, Paris. *Chester Dale Collection*, 1962. Signed, and dated 1873, and exhibited in the Salon of 1873. Canvas, 24¼ x 20″ (61.5 x 51 cm.).

Vincent van Gogh

(DUTCH, 1853–1890)

98   LA MOUSMÉ

Cézanne was not the only artist to react against Impressionism, against its absorption in the facts of vision. Van Gogh also wished to escape the Impressionist tyranny of the eye, to go beyond the mere transcriptions of appearance. A study of Japanese prints liberated him. From them he learned to paint in masses of flat tone or masses of but slightly broken color, and to treat the picture surface as decoration.

Van Gogh wrote his brother, Theo, "I envy the Japanese the extreme clearness which everything has in their work. It is never tedious, and never seems to be done too hurriedly. Their work is as simple as breathing, and they do a figure in a few sure strokes with the same ease as if it were as simple as buttoning your coat." But van Gogh never attained this facility. He wrote again in July 1888 of *La Mousmé*, "It took me a whole week, I have not been able to do anything else, not having been very well either . . . but I had to reserve my mental energy to do the *mousmé* well. A *mousmé* is a Japanese girl—Provencal in this case—12 to 14 years old." Creation was easier for the Japanese artist. He was a member of a group, where everyone worked in the same tradition, but van Gogh was a lonely individual, never sure of his way, only certain that he must follow his self-destroying search for beauty. It was a quest that cost him first his sanity and then his life, but he knew in the end that he had found the Grail he sought.

Collections: Mme J. van Gogh-Bonger, Amsterdam; Carl Sternheim, La Hulpe, Belgium; Alphonse Kann, St.-Germain-en-Laye, France; J. B. Stang, Oslo. *Chester Dale Collection*, 1962. Painted 1888. Canvas, 28⅞ x 23¾" (73.4 x 60 cm.).

Paul Gauguin

(FRENCH, 1848–1903)

99 FATATA TE MITI

Paul Gauguin, when already a man of middle age, abandoned his prosperous brokerage business, his wife and children, and ultimately all civilized life to devote himself to painting. Some demon of creativity drove him toward an exotic world, first to Panama, where he worked as a digger on the canal, then to Martinique, where the climate nearly killed him, and finally, after seventeen months of poverty in France, to the tropics again, first to Tahiti and later to the Marquesas and a solitary death at La Dominique.

The picture reproduced here, dated 1892, was painted a few months after Gauguin's first arrival at Tahiti. Disgusted with the European character of life at Papeete, he had withdrawn to the interior of the island to live among the natives. Tehura, a Polynesian of great beauty, became his *vahine* and probably posed for the figure of the girl on the right removing her sarong.

It was during these brief halcyon days that Gauguin developed his theories of the analogy of color to music. "Are not these repetitions of tone," he was later to ask, "these monotonous color harmonies (in the musical sense) analogous to Oriental chants sung in a shrill voice, to the accompaniment of pulsating notes which intensify them by contrast?"

In all his canvases painted in the South Seas, complementary colors—orange and blue, yellow and violet, green and red—at their highest intensities and without modulation of values, are balanced harmoniously against each other, forming beautiful, almost abstract patterns. *Fatata te Miti*, which means "by the sea," is a masterpiece of the painter's newly created style, in which he uses colors as arbitrarily as a composer uses sound. It may have been this picture which Mallarmé, the symbolist poet, had in mind when he said of a canvas by his friend Gauguin, "It is a musical poem, it needs no libretto."

Collections: Ambroise Vollard, Paris; Louis Horch, New York. *Chester Dale Collection*, 1962. Signed, and dated 1892. Canvas, 26¾ x 36" (68 x 91.5 cm.).

Fatou te Miti

P. Gauguin

Henri de Toulouse-Lautrec

(FRENCH, 1864–1901)

100   A CORNER OF THE MOULIN DE LA GALETTE

The Moulin de la Galette was for Toulouse-Lautrec a favorite haunt, a catchall of the types he liked to paint. It was an unpretentious wineshop, which still survives near the summit of Montmartre. On certain days it was frequented by petty gangsters and streetwalkers, on other days by a more conservative set. Lautrec in the picture reproduced here seems to have painted the less rowdy clientele. Catching them in a moment of repose, he has drawn the bourgeois men and women with the utmost simplicity and without his usual distortions.

It is a brilliant composition. The casual juxtaposition of seven figures is seized on to form an intricately balanced design. Although only four faces are clearly seen, the mood of each of the seven is conveyed, even of the tall man whose head is so daringly cut by the frame. The edge of the face of the woman seen from behind suggests her smile; the toss of the next woman's head carries its invitation; the sideburn of the man with the beret gives his character; the fixed and purposeless gaze of the three central figures in the foreground suggests their dreary tragedy of boredom. It is also a profound painting, a masterly study in loneliness. The figures are crowded together in space but isolated in their own thoughts. No one looks at anyone else. Our attention is focused on the young girl standing in the center behind a table. In spite of her ugly, mannish clothes, she has a latent beauty rarely found in Lautrec's women.

In stature she seems hardly more than a child but with a face prematurely lined and saddened. Did Lautrec glimpse for a moment a woman perfectly formed but almost of his own size, someone else who knew what it was to make observations among elbows? Lautrec had a passionate nature and was in constant search of affection—not friendship only, for which he had a genius, but something deeper and more intimate. In his treatment of this tired, dispirited, but still beautiful woman one feels a mood of sympathy, even of tenderness. There is an overtone which almost approaches compassion and which, combined with Lautrec's other qualities of incisive vision, makes the *Moulin de la Galette* one of his greatest achievements, a masterpiece of nineteenth-century painting.

Collections: Depeaux; Gerstenberg, Berlin. *Chester Dale Collection*, 1962. Signed, and dated 1892. Cardboard mounted on wood, 39½ x 35⅛" (100.3 x 89.1 cm.).

Thomas Eakins

(AMERICAN, 1844-1916)

101 THE BIGLIN BROTHERS RACING

Thomas Eakins was the most intellectual artist America has produced, and yet *The Biglin Brothers Racing*, which he painted probably in 1873, looks at first glance as fortuitous and casual as a colored snapshot. Where did the intellectual element in Eakins' painting show itself? What is the difference between a realistic painting of this kind and a good color photograph? Although Eakins himself was a pioneer photographer, he used the camera only as a mechanical means of gathering data about appearance, not as a basis for his pictures. This scene of a rowing race about to begin, for example, was put together in the studio from sketches and from memory. The picture seems photographic because painter and camera have the same goal, to show, as Eakins said, "What o'clock it is, afternoon or morning, winter or summer, and what kind of people are there, and what they are doing and why they are doing it."

But these facts the painter can convey more convincingly than the camera. A photograph taken on a sunny day indicates sunshine; but Eakins' careful study of reflected light taught him how to exaggerate the sparkle of sunlight on water until the waves seemed to catch the rays of the sun itself. A photograph indicates depth but Eakins' precise perspective, worked out mathematically, draws the spectator's vision into this depth, makes him part of the scene. And a photograph sometimes fixes in the kaleidoscope of appearance a satisfactory design; but it almost never achieves, as in *The Biglin Brothers Racing*, an integrated composition in which no object can be altered or removed without destroying the whole effect.

Collections: Mrs. Thomas Eakins; Whitney Museum of American Art, New York. *Gift of Mr. and Mrs. Cornelius Vanderbilt Whitney*, 1953. Painted probably 1873. Canvas, 24 x 36 " (61 x 91.5 cm.).

Winslow Homer

(AMERICAN, 1836-1910)

102   BREEZING UP

The distinguished achievement of American painting in the second half of the nineteenth century was due in no small part to Winslow Homer, who shares with Thomas Eakins a preeminent position in the tradition of American realism. Homer was trained as an illustrator, and an element of illustration appears in his pictures from beginning to end. His earliest significant work was drawn for *Harper's Weekly* during the Civil War, when he was detailed to the Army of the Potomac as a correspondent. Working for a magazine, he learned to make his illustrations clear and specific. Throughout his life he presented his subjects graphically and made them appear to exist convincingly. Such objective recording has now almost vanished from art; and Homer's pictorial style with its simple, lucid statements has had little if any influence in recent years.

Yet Homer was able to suggest mood, feeling, atmosphere, as vividly as any Abstract Expressionist. Three small boys and a fisherman in a sailboat evoke the pleasure of sailing before a fair breeze; a dory with men peering over the side into a foggy sky conveys the loneliness and vastness of the sea; a huntsman with his dog silhouetted against the mountain suggests the exhilaration of sport. One could elaborate endlessly.

But the important point is that a certain mood is induced in the spectator's mind by recognizable images. Representation in the visual arts is, of course, traditional. The basic language of painting with rare exceptions has always been representational, an imagery of identifiable objects. At times, however, painting has tried to usurp the function of other arts: poetry, for example, with the Pre-Raphaelites, and music with the Abstract Expressionists. With Winslow Homer, there is no confusion of the arts. He simply represents actual scenes with such vividness, with such grasp of significance, that their pervading mood is inescapable.

Collections: Charles Stewart Smith, New York; Howard Caswell Smith, Oyster Bay, New York. *Gift of the W. L. and May T. Mellon Foundation*, 1943. Signed, and dated 1876. Canvas, 24⅛ x 38⅛" (61.5 x 97 cm.).

James McNeill Whistler

(AMERICAN, 1834-1903)

103   THE WHITE GIRL (SYMPHONY IN WHITE, NO. 1)

There have always been two opposed traditions in American painting. Eakins and Homer represent one: a rugged, native vitality; Whistler and Mary Cassatt illustrate the second: a genteel, Europeanized urbanity. Although Whistler's fame is brighter in Europe than in America, his sophisticated selection of what seems best, wherever found, is of exceptional significance to this country, for it marks the coming of age of American painting.

Whistler would never have understood or approved of Homer's or Eakins' works. He tried to avoid what they sought, qualities he described as "damned realism, and beautiful nature and the whole mess." He preached a return to "that wondrous thing called the masterpiece, which surpasses in perfection all that they [the gods] have contrived in what is called Nature." In other words, Whistler wished to demonstrate that the inventive force of the artist is more important than the recording power of his eye. To do this he combined the patterns of Japanese prints with that mastery of value relations which distinguishes the painting of Velázquez. This eclecticism is predictable from even so early a work as *The White Girl*, a portrait of his mistress Joanna Heffernan. It was shown in 1863 at the Salon des Refusés with what we now consider to be many of the finest French paintings of the second half of the nineteenth century. It proved to be the sensation of that exhibition, the most revolutionary held in France in a hundred years.

True, the public was hostile, and Zola has reported how people nudged one another and became almost hysterical with laughter in front of the painting. But the wisest connoisseurs and critics were enthusiastic, and with *The White Girl* Whistler became the first American painter since the eighteenth century to attain renown and leadership among European artists.

Collection: Thomas Whistler, Baltimore. *Harris Whittemore Collection,* 1943. Signed, and dated 1862. Canvas, 84½ x 42½" (214.7 x 108 cm.).

John Singer Sargent

(AMERICAN, 1856–1925)

104 MRS. ADRIAN ISELIN

Sargent's painting of Mrs. Iselin epitomizes the American mothers described in the novels of Henry James: ruthless guardians of their young, determined managers of financial and social advancement. Thirty years after Sargent had painted this portrait he was asked if he remembered it. He thought for a moment before he replied, "Of course! I cannot forget that dominating little finger." And with what skill he has shown it tapping the edge of the table!

Mrs. Iselin's grandson has recounted how reluctant she was to have her portrait painted. When Sargent came for the first sitting, she entered the room in an extremely irritated manner, followed by her maid carrying her best French frocks, and haughtily told the artist to choose a dress. Sargent replied that he wanted to paint her just as she was. He did not mention that he intended to portray her resentful expression at having to pose, her air of contempt for the painter, and her large and ugly ear.

In those early days the young portraitist was more courageous and less bored than he would become in later years. He painted his sitters as he saw them, disregarding their feelings and their wishes. He was at his best when the character and the mood he wanted to portray were obvious. Mrs. Iselin was a perfect model. She was firm, self-confident, perhaps a little aggressive. One admires her without feeling the least sympathy for her forceful personality, which Sargent has caught unforgettably.

Technically the painting is brilliant, but it reveals the flaw which Henry James astutely perceived and described in an essay published the year before the portrait was painted. After praising Sargent's astounding dexterity, the novelist asked, "Yes, but what is left?" He observed that "it may be better for an artist to have a certain part of his property invested in unsolved difficulties." And he concluded his essay saying, "The highest result [in portraiture] is achieved when to this element of quick perception a certain faculty of brooding reflection is added." This "faculty of brooding reflection" was exactly what Sargent lacked, and as a consequence his work for all its brio remains superficial.

Collections: Family of the sitter, New York City and New Rochelle. *Gift of Ernest Iselin*, 1964. Signed, and dated 1888. Canvas, 60½ x 36⅝" (153.7 x 93 cm.).

105

106

Mary Cassatt (American, 1844–1926)

105 *Girl Arranging Her Hair.* 1886. Canvas, 29½ x 24½″ (75 x 62.3 cm.). Chester Dale Collection

106 *Portrait of an Elderly Lady.* c. 1887. Canvas, 28⅝ x 23¾″ (72.7 x 60.4 cm.). Chester Dale Collection

107 *The Loge.* Signed. 1882. Canvas, 31⅜ x 25⅛″ (79.7 x 63.8 cm.). Chester Dale Collection

108 *Miss Mary Ellison.* Signed. c. 1880. Canvas, 33½ x 25¾″ (84.8 x 65.3 cm.). Chester Dale Collection

109 *Woman with a Red Zinnia.* Signed. 1891. Canvas, 29 x 23¾″ (74 x 60.4 cm.). Chester Dale Collection

110 *Two Children at the Seashore.* Canvas, 38½ x 29¼″ (98 x 74.5 cm.). Ailsa Mellon Bruce Collection

107

08

109

110

Mary Cassatt, like her friend Degas, studied the old masters assiduously. This is evident in *Girl Arranging Her Hair*, which was shown in 1886 in the last Impressionist exhibition. Miss Cassatt has taken an awkward adolescent and placed her in the pose of Michelangelo's *Bound Slave*, a statue she had often seen in the Louvre. Degas, entranced with her blending of the contemporary and the classical, bought the painting and kept it until he died. But the picture is not characteristic of Miss Cassatt's work. More in her usual style is *The Loge*. It shows her particular qualities: an elaborate and fragile refinement, a mood of social fastidiousness, which suggests the novels of her fellow expatriates Henry James and Edith Wharton.

Edouard Vuillard

(FRENCH, 1868–1940)

111 THÉODORE DURET

Vuillard was at his best when he was exploring the increasing frailty and infirmity of age. He seems to have felt a tender sympathy for those who were on the downward slope of life, and repeatedly painted them as they hastened onward at an ineluctably faster speed. He observed his mother in scores of paintings, noting her face with its ever deepening lines; her back bending more and more, from rheumatism; the gradual graying of her hair; and her growing resemblance to his grandmother, whom he drew when he was a young man.

Old men equally fascinated him. His likeness of Théodore Duret, the art critic and champion of the Impressionists, is among the most sensitive representations of age since the late portraits of Rembrandt. Duret sits in his study, surrounded by his works of art. Directly behind him are three paintings, the smaller ones unidentified, the larger one, *Telemachus and Mentor* by Tiepolo, now belonging to the Rijksmuseum, Amsterdam. Reflected in the mirror is Duret's portrait by Whistler, later acquired by the Metropolitan Museum, New York. In Whistler's painting, Duret is shown carrying over his arm a pink cloak, which is the key to Vuillard's own color scheme, and in his hand an opera hat. He looks a typical boulevardier. Thirty years pass, and Duret has totally changed. He appears meager; his hands seem to tremble; his eyes are red rimmed. His weightless, insubstantial body is rendered no more definitely than his surroundings. Thus this apparition of old age dissolves into its chromatic constituents, takes on the protective coloration characteristic of Vuillard's figures, and becomes one substance with all the other details of the scene. There is an effect of imprecision, enhanced by the use of cardboard as a ground. Because of its absorbency, outlines are blurred, and the result is a uniformity of texture, which Vuillard loved.

That nothing is precisely seen does not affect the precision of the design. The carefully constructed composition defines the mood of the portrait. Vuillard wished to indicate the claustral life of a scholar. Consequently Duret is shown as tightly constricted by the angles of the desk piled high with books, papers, reviews, the paraphernalia of his trade. The two wings of the writing table are like the blades of a scissors, seemingly ready to sheer the sitter in two, to destroy him. His favorite cat, Lulu, sits on his knee, an intimation of his solitude, his loneliness. It is a masterpiece of psychological portraiture; as Claude Roger-Marx has said, it "is worthy of inclusion with the great portraits of writers at work—with the Zola of Manet, the Duranty of Degas, and the Gustave Geffroy of Cézanne."

Collection: Théodore Duret, Paris. *Chester Dale Collection,* 1962. Signed, and dated 1912. Cardboard mounted on wood, 37½ x 29½" (95.2 x 74.8 cm.).

Amedeo Modigliani

(ITALIAN, 1884–1920)

112   CHAIM SOUTINE

If I were asked to choose the greatest portrait painter of the twentieth century, I would unhesitatingly pick Modigliani. For he has solved beyond any of his contemporaries the basic problem of portraiture: how to represent the human face both as a likeness of an individual and as an element of formal design. His entire life was devoted to this study. Other artists painted still lifes, figure compositions, landscapes, but Modigliani restricted himself virtually to portraiture. Even his rare and beautiful nudes are essentially portraits of the model.

To combine a formal stylization with a telling likeness, this was the goal of the great Renaissance masters, who were his heroes. Modigliani would have been accepted into their Pantheon, whereas Sargent would have been rejected. Take, for example, the portrait of Chaim Soutine. The sitter is rendered in Modigliani's highly idiomatic style as a formal pattern within the rectangle of the canvas, but if one compares the portrait with a photograph of the artist, one realizes how successful Modigliani has been in catching the curious dichotomy of his appearance: that of an uncouth peasant with a thick nose and coarse, asymmetrical features, joined to a sensitive artist with slender wrists and tapering fingers.

Modigliani also did a drawing of Soutine now in a Los Angeles collection. It has the beautiful rhythm of lines he always attained, but it is less convincing as a likeness. When he came to paint a portrait he scrutinized his sitter more carefully. He stressed the distinctive features of his model: in this case his friend's long neck, his broad nostrils, his black, unruly hair, and his clasped hands, suggestive of insecurity and of an underlying diffidence.

Between the two artists there must have been a deep affinity. Both were drawn to Paris, one from Lithuania, the other from Italy. Both were Jewish, Soutine the son of an indigent mender of clothes, Modigliani of a middle-class stockbroker and dealer in hides and coal. Both knew extreme poverty, and both were kept from starvation by the same Polish picture peddler, Zborowski, who tried tirelessly to sell their paintings to the more important dealers. But Modigliani did not have Soutine's peasant physique. Destitution, combined with alcohol and drugs, killed him at thirty-six. Jean Cocteau has described seeing him on the terrace outside the Rotonde always drawing people's faces. He reminded the poet "of the proud contemptuous gypsies, who sit down at your table and read your hand . . . Modigliani did not paint to order, and he exaggerated his drunkenness, his outbursts of fury, and his incongruous laughter as a defense against [those] who were offended by his haughtiness."

Collections: Léopold Zborowski, Paris; Jacques Netter, Paris. *Chester Dale Collection*, 1962. Signed. Painted 1917. Canvas, 36⅛ x 23½" (91.7 x 59.7 cm.).

153

Georges Braque

(FRENCH, 1882-1963)

113 NUDE WOMAN WITH BASKET OF FRUIT

Braque's father and grandfather were housepainters, and he learned from them the meaning of craftsmanship. They gave him his command of texture, and above all they taught him patience and perseverance. He was always slow but determined. He used to box with Derain, and he would wear him down with a ponderous and impenetrable defense until his more powerful but wilder opponent could be felled with a single well-aimed blow. This tenacious slowness was characteristic of Braque's approach to painting. As he said, "Progress in art consists not in extending one's limits, but in knowing them better."

His fortieth birthday occurred in 1922, when the Salon d'Automne held a special exhibition in recognition of his achievement. The same year, at the height of his powers, he began his series of Canephori (Ceremonial Basket Bearers). Sensuality as we find it in the Old Masters, the late works of Titian and Rubens, for example, is difficult, though not impossible, to combine with the increasing abstraction characteristic of contemporary painting. And yet Braque's monumental, partially draped figures, abstract as they are, have a compelling eroticism that is impossible to forget. The giantess reproduced here might well represent "wide-bosomed Earth, the everlasting foundation of us all," as John Russell has pointed out, or conjure up "member-loving Aphrodite." In either role she suggests some modern symbol of fertility.

But the remarkable fact is the way these two-dimensional goddesses with their deliquescent outlines seem to have a visionary existence. Although nothing is modeled and there is no deviation from the flatness of the *espace pictural*, yet skillfully selected color patches and brilliantly related contours suggest volume, so that one can easily imagine the figures translated into sculpture, statues such as one sees in the gardens of Versailles. Apollinaire once said, "No one is less concerned than he [Braque] with psychology, and I fancy a stone moves him as much as a face does." Such indifference to personality led him to create universal types of femininity.

The series of the Canephori ended around 1927. According to Jean Leymarie, "Among many variants of unequal value, some less firmly designed than others, though all are imbued with a decorative stateliness, the finest is the Canephorus of 1926 in the Chester Dale Collection in Washington, outstanding for its power and robust vigour." And also, I might add, for its amplitude and fluidity of form.

Collection: Paul Rosenberg, Paris. *Chester Dale Collection*, 1962. Signed, and dated 1926. Canvas, 63¾ x 29¼" (162 x 74.3 cm.).

114

115

116

117

Henri Matisse (French, 1869–1954)

114 *Pot of Geraniums*. Signed. 1912. Canvas, 16¼ x 13⅛" (41.3 x 33.3 cm.). Chester Dale Collection

115 *Still Life with Pineapple*. Signed. 1924. Canvas, 19⅞ x 24¼" (50.5 x 61.5 cm.). Gift of the W. Averell Harriman Foundation in memory of Marie N. Harriman

116 *Woman with Amphora and Pomegranates*. 1952. Paper on canvas (collage), 96 x 37⅞" (243.6 x 96.3 cm.). Ailsa Mellon Bruce Fund

117 *Les Gorges du Loup*. Signed. 1920/25. Canvas, 19¾ x 24" (50.2 x 60.9 cm.). Chester Dale Collection

118 *La Coiffure*. Signed. 1901. Canvas, 37½ x 31½" (95.2 x 80.1 cm.). Chester Dale Collection

119 *Odalisque with Raised Arms*. Signed. 1923. Canvas, 25⅝ x 19¾" (65.1 x 50.2 cm.). Chester Dale Collection

120 *Venus*. Signed with initials. 1952. Paper on canvas (collage), 39⅞ x 30⅛" (101.2 x 76.5 cm.). Ailsa Mellon Bruce Fund

121 *Still Life: Apples on Pink Tablecloth*. Signed. c. 1922. Canvas, 23¾ x 28¾" (60.4 x 73 cm.). Chester Dale Collection

18

119

Matisse's painting bears a superficial and deceptive resemblance to the work of a child. But the revolution he introduced into art is rooted in studies which began when he was a copyist in the Louvre, and which he continued to do through his last years, when he executed his greatest designs—for a Dominican chapel at Vence, in southern France. Like Michelangelo, however, Matisse was always at pains to hide the effort that had gone into his work. He wished his paintings "to have the lightness and joyousness of springtime, which never lets anyone suspect the labor it has cost." In this statement he described his greatest gift: almost alone among twentieth-century artists he was able to convey his own delight in a person, or a place, or a flower, to communicate a joyousness of vision which eighty-five years and two wars did not diminish.

120

121

Pablo Picasso

(SPANISH, 1881–1973)

122 FAMILY OF SALTIMBANQUES

In 1905 Picasso intended to paint two large pictures but completed only one, the *Family of Saltimbanques*. Roughly seven feet square, it is the most impressive achievement of his early period. His many studies of the friends he had made at the Cirque Medrano—clowns, jugglers, and strolling players—are here gathered together in an empty, treeless landscape under a blue sky from which a fog seems to be clearing. On one side is a group comprising Harlequin holding the hand of a little girl, next to him the director of the troupe with a heavy paunch, dressed in red tights and wearing the mock crown of the bronze jester sculptured at about the same time, and at his side two adolescent acrobats. The composition is balanced precariously by a solitary girl (inspired perhaps by a Tanagra statuette), who is seated further in the foreground. These detached figures are unified by their mood of contemplation and by their inner loneliness.

Harlequin has the profile of Picasso himself. Jung has pointed out that the artist's desire to paint himself repeatedly in this disguise reveals a subconscious wish to play the role of Harlequin, "to juggle with everything," as Roland Penrose has perceptively said, "while remaining aloof and irresponsible."

The enigma of these circus people standing together as though awaiting some command or some mysterious event fascinated the German poet Rainer Maria Rilke. In 1918 he asked a friend who owned the painting whether he might live in the same room with it. Later he told her that the *Saltimbanques*, "the loveliest Picasso in which there is so much Paris that for moments I forget," had inspired him to write the fifth of his *Duino Elegies*, which begins:

> But tell me, who *are* they, these acrobats, even a little
> more fleeting than we ourselves—so urgently, ever since childhood,
> wrung by an (oh, for the sake of whom?)
> never-contented will? That keeps on wringing them,
> bending them, slinging them, swinging them,
> throwing them and catching them back; as though from an oily
> smoother air, they come down on the threadbare
> carpet, thinned by their everlasting
> upspringing, this carpet forlornly
> lost in the cosmos.

Collections: André Level, Paris; "Peau de l'Ours," Paris; Hertha von Koenig, Munich. *Chester Dale Collection*, 1962. Signed. Painted 1905. Canvas, 83¾ x 90⅜" (212.8 x 229.6 cm.).

Index

All numbers in this Index refer to *plates* and *commentaries*.